1991

Continuing Edu
in the Year 2000

Ralph G. Brockett, *Editor*
Montana State University

NEW DIRECTIONS FOR CONTINUING EDUCATION

GORDON G. DARKENWALD, *Editor-in-Chief*
Rutgers University

ALAN B. KNOX, *Consulting Editor*
University of Wisconsin

Number 36, Winter 1987

Paperback sourcebooks in
The Jossey-Bass Higher Education Series

Jossey-Bass Inc., Publishers
San Francisco • London

Ralph G. Brockett (ed.).
Continuing Education in the Year 2000.
New Directions for Continuing Education, no. 36.
San Francisco: Jossey-Bass, 1987.

New Directions for Continuing Education
Gordon G. Darkenwald, *Editor-in-Chief*
Alan B. Knox, *Consulting Editor*

New Directions for Continuing Education is published quarterly
by Jossey-Bass Inc., Publishers (publication number USPS 493-930).
Second-class postage paid at San Francisco, California, and at
additional mailing offices. POSTMASTER: Send address changes to
Jossey-Bass Inc., Publishers, 433 California Street, San Francisco,
California 94104.

Editorial correspondence should be sent to the Editor-in-Chief,
Gordon G. Darkenwald, Graduate School of Education, Rutgers
University, 10 Seminary Place, New Brunswick, New Jersey 08903.

Library of Congress Catalog Card Number LC 85-644750

International Standard Serial Number ISSN 0195-2242

International Standard Book Number ISBN 1-55542-950-5

Cover art by WILLI BAUM

Manufactured in the United States of America

Ordering Information

The paperback sourcebooks listed below are published quarterly and can be ordered either by subscription or single copy.

Subscriptions cost $48.00 per year for institutions, agencies, and libraries. Individuals can subscribe at the special rate of $36.00 per year *if payment is by personal check.* (Note that the full rate of $48.00 applies if payment is by institutional check, even if the subscription is designated for an individual.) Standing orders are accepted.

Single copies are available at $11.95 when payment accompanies order. (California, New Jersey, New York, and Washington, D.C., residents please include appropriate sales tax.) For billed orders, cost per copy is $11.95 plus postage and handling.

Substantial discounts are offered to organizations and individuals wishing to purchase bulk quantities of Jossey-Bass sourcebooks. Please inquire.

Please note that these prices are for the academic year 1987–88 and are subject to change without notice. Also, some titles may be out of print and therefore not available for sale.

To ensure correct and prompt delivery, all orders must give either the *name of an individual* or an *official purchase order number.* Please submit your order as follows:

Subscriptions: specify series and year subscription is to begin.
Single Copies: specify sourcebook code (such as, CE1) and first two words of title.

Mail orders for United States and Possessions, Australia, New Zealand, Canada, Latin America, and Japan to:
Jossey-Bass Inc., Publishers
433 California Street
San Francisco, California 94104

Mail orders for all other parts of the world to:
Jossey-Bass Limited
28 Banner Street
London EC1Y 8QE

New Directions for Continuing Education Series
Gordon G. Darkenwald, *Editor-in-Chief*
Alan B. Knox, *Consulting Editor*

Contents

Editor's Notes

What will the field of continuing education look like in the year 2000? To a large extent, the answer to this question will come from those practicing in the field today. While it is likely that the need for continuing education opportunities will continue to expand in the coming years, the success of these efforts will be determined, to a large degree, by the ability of continuing educators to play an active role in planning for the future.

Continuing education has, historically, had a strong future orientation. Numerous books, monographs, articles, conferences, and courses—particularly during the past two decades—have been devoted to the future of continuing education. The purpose of this sourcebook is to draw from current practice and research in order to offer a vision of the field in the relatively near future as seen through the eyes of continuing educators who, as practitioners and researchers, are currently making a contribution to that future.

In Chapter One, Hiemstra sets the stage for exploring the future by reviewing the evolution of continuing education in this century and exploring how the past and present can be used to provide insight into the future. He argues that educators of adults can and must play an active role in shaping the future of the field. The context for continuing education in the year 2000 is examined in Chapter Two by Fay, McCune, and Begin, who identify larger societal trends and their implications for continuing education.

Brockett and Darkenwald, in Chapter Three, offer an examination of research on the adult learner. By looking at several current research areas and issues, they project some likely directions for the study of the adult learner in the years to come. As is true within the larger society, technology is almost certain to have a major impact on the future of continuing education. Garrison explores some of these prospects in Chapter Four. Smith, in Chapter Five, shifts the focus to the continuing educator by examining issues in the management of continuing education programs in the next century. And in Chapter Six, Cervero shares a vision of how the issue of professionalization may affect the field by the turn of the century.

How can continuing educators work to achieve the kinds of directions envisioned by the above authors? Deshler, in Chapter Seven, presents several techniques based on such approaches as projection, forecasting, prevention, adaptation, invention, and creation to help continuing educators play an active role in creating the future. In the final

1

chapter, Brockett provides a brief summary of the preceding chapters and points out that while the future will witness many changes, diversity and controversy will likely continue to be hallmarks of the field.

Continuing education as a professional field of study and practice is a development of the twentieth century. As we approach the year 2000, we need to begin planning for the directions we would like the field to take in the coming years. We can choose to deny the future, ignore it, or embrace it and work to shape it. The authors of this sourcebook are committed to the belief that only through the latter approach will the field be able to achieve its greatest potential.

Ralph G. Brockett
Editor

*Ralph G. Brockett is assistant professor of adult education
at the Center for Adult Learning Research, Montana State
University, Bozeman, Montana. He has worked in continuing
education for health and human services professionals, served
on the executive committee of the Commission of Professors
of Adult Education, and is currently book review editor for*
Adult Education Quarterly.

Continuing educators can and must play a role in shaping the future of the field. Some future roles for continuing educators can be projected.

Creating the Future

Roger Hiemstra

Why should we think about the future? Should the professional who must worry about that upcoming task for next week or whether the budget will be overrun this month also be future oriented? Can anything be done to prepare for the future as professional continuing educators? Questions such as these must be raised and answered in order to success-fully meet the challenges that come with future change. This chapter will provide some arguments as to why continuing educators can and must play a role in shaping their own futures.

One argument stems from the consciousness-raising efforts of authors like Bell (1968, 1973), Toffler (1970, 1980), Theobald (1972), and Naisbitt (1982), who have helped many educators consider the rapidity and constancy of change as an issue that affects them throughout life. The resultant problems with which people must deal—such as a mobile society, job obsolescence, ever increasing numbers of homeless and hun-gry throughout the world, and the difficulties that many are having cop-ing with such change—present some real challenges for continuing educators, both personally and professionally.

Another argument deals with the value of learning throughout life as a mechanism for coping with changes that the future inevitably brings. For example, some experts believe that the apex of improving life conditions is near or may already have been reached. Such signposts as scarce resources, world turmoil, and the seemingly ever enlarging "have-

R. G. Brockett (ed.). *Continuing Education in the Year 2000.*
New Directions for Continuing Education, no. 36. San Francisco: Jossey-Bass, Winter 1987.

nots" group are quite visible with today's worldwide communications networks (Ross-Macdonald, Hassell, and McNeill, 1977). Thus, positive attitudes regarding the value of learning throughout life, a willingness to deal with crucial problems that come with advanced understanding, and an ability to anticipate, plan for, and even create the future may perhaps be the only means for making decisions that will benefit society in positive ways.

Determining exactly what the future will be so that correct decisions can be made is not easy because there often is an unlimited number of future paths down which to travel. Several futurists suggest that the options are fairly restricted, based on rational extrapolations of past trends. Thus, one prediction is that the world will continue to become technotronic in nature, with electronic gadgetry, instant communications, laser-based technology, and robotic substitutions for much of today's manual labor requirements. Another version is based on the belief that the world is racing toward a postindustrial crash where scarcity of natural resources and a crush of constant population expansion will result in worldwide upheaval of current governmental structures and divisions. A few even suggest that some sort of nuclear-related conflict or accident will create such dire environmental problems that our ability to cope with life will be greatly reduced.

This chapter is based on a notion that the future will not be at an extreme of any of these rather pessimistic predictions. It is believed we will continue to find a middle ground, although there certainly are various options still open to people throughout the world. Finding such a central path depends, perhaps optimistically, on rational uses of technological development, wise expenditures of available resources, control of population expansion, and finding peaceful solutions to tensions existing between today's superpowers (Bell and Mau, 1971; Jungk, 1976; Roszak, 1979).

Realistically, such faith must be matched by a willingness of world leaders, both politicians and wealth holders, to make several crucial decisions over the next few years. Whatever paths world leaders take, continuous learning on the part of all citizens will be required if sensible options are to be determined, studied, and chosen (Ziegler, 1970; Toffler, 1974; Wagschal and Kahn, 1979). Continuing educators must play an important role in such activity, and shaping the future as professionals is vital if they are to do a good job.

Past to the Present

Continuing educators actually have been shaping their futures for many years. This chapter is not an appropriate vehicle for any thorough tracing of adult and continuing education's rich history. The reader is referred to such sources as Grattan (1955), Verner (1967), Knowles (1977), Taylor, Rockhill, and Fieldhouse (1985) if a comprehensive background on this history is desired. However, it needs to be said that the growing involvement of adults in organized learning activities during the seventeenth and eighteenth centuries in North America and throughout the world was an indication that many people wished to control some of their own destinies through enhanced abilities. Benjamin Franklin's "Junto," university outreach programs for adults, Josiah Holbrook's "Lyceums," and various public institutions such as libraries and museums were all initiated during this time period.

The close of the eighteenth century saw continuing education begin to move from what was primarily a religious or localized orientation to some formats stimulated by the advance of industrialization. In Great Britain, for example, there was concern for the poor, and many began to learn to read in evening schools. Mechanics' Institutions were being established in many towns throughout England by early in the nineteenth century to meet some educational needs of working-class people. In Denmark, N.F.S. Grundtvig created the folk high school where farmers and artisans could become aware of their country's rich heritage. In the United States, John Vincent helped to establish the Chautauqua Institution, which included resident courses at Chautauqua Lake in the state of New York on a variety of topics and a subsequent progeny of traveling tent shows where lecturers, entertainment, and culture were brought to people throughout much of the country.

The beginning of the twentieth century saw some new forms of continuing education evolve. The Agricultural Extension Service, later known primarily as the Cooperative Extension Service, was born in 1914, resulting in an organization that provided a variety of educational opportunities to rural people throughout the United States. Several other aspects of adult and continuing education, still relevant today, began about this time: the discovery of the adult as a learner in terms of research, the training and professionalization of continuing educators, a need for adult literacy and vocational training programs, and the marketing of continuing education programs.

My purpose in presenting this brief synopsis of historical information is to accent a belief that some understanding of continuing education's evolution is necessary if we are to fully appreciate the value in looking at our future. Our history shapes our future, and projecting into this future cannot be done in isolation from either our past or our present.

History of "Futures" Activity

There has been considerable interest in future projection activities during the past two decades. In fact, this interest has developed into a field of study involving the development of a body of literature, evolution of research and projecting techniques (Henley and Yates, 1974; Fowles, 1978), creation of professional associations of futurists, and teaching of college courses on future studies. The most complete clearinghouse of futures-related material is the World Future Society (located at 4916 Saint Elmo Avenue, Bethesda, Maryland 20814). This organization gathers material and information on a wide variety of categories, and the interested reader can obtain a catalogue of materials from them.

Continuing educators, too, have been involved in various futures activities. Several graduate programs of adult and continuing education in North America and elsewhere offer courses related to projecting the future. Journal articles, books, and dissertations with future studies themes have been written by continuing educators. For example, Ilsley (1982) wrote an award-winning dissertation on the relevance of the future for adult and continuing educators, and Harrington (1977) wrote a book entitled *The Future of Adult Education*.

There also have been some special futures invention activities involving continuing educators during the past fifteen years (Marien and Ziegler, 1972; Glover, 1979). For instance, several continuing educators have been trained in future projection techniques (such as scenario writing, the Delphi technique, cross-impact study, and trend extrapolation) and have facilitated workshops in various locations to help continuing education professionals and students better understand and have an impact on their future. These are addressed in greater detail by Deshler in Chapter Seven. There also have been state or region-wide workshops in the United States that have focused on future-related topics of interest. One such workshop was "Future of Adult Education and Learning Projects" in the state of Washington that examined the future of citizen participation (Kaplan, 1976). Several similar projects were sponsored by the former U.S. Office of Education and administered by the Educational Policy Research Center of Syracuse, New York, on such subjects as adult education, lifelong learning, policy development, and futures invention (Healy, 1979).

Perhaps the most ambitious effort of this sort was the 1973–74 National Adult Education Think Tank Project coordinated by Hanberry (1975) and funded by the U.S. Office of Education. Professional continuing educators, governmental policymakers, part-time continuing education teachers, and adult students participated in a series of regional workshops and one national workshop to develop policy, outline programming needs, and generally dream about the field's future. Ideas developed in the project, discussions with political leaders, published materials by several participants (Delker, 1974; Ohliger, 1974; Hiemstra, 1976; Gross, 1977), and influences from the work of people throughout the world (Himmelstrup, 1980) led to the 1976 Lifelong Learning Act (Public

Law 94–482) as Title I, Part B, of the amendments to the Higher Education Act of 1965. The act received initial monies for study and development, facilitating the establishment of an office in Washington, D.C., promoting widespread discussion, and enabling several reports and papers to be published. Although final funding money was not obtained, perhaps because of narrow definitions and interpretations, the act had a widespread impact on the field. Cassara (1979) presents some helpful reflections on the Lifelong Learning Act and its impact.

I was fortunate enough to have participated in the Think Tank project. The experience created for all participants a sense of the power in understanding future possibilities and in being able to think creatively about what that understanding can mean. It provided evidence that continuing educators can and must play a role in shaping the future.

In concluding this section, it is important to note that the Commission of Professors of Adult Education, although not necessarily carrying out futures invention activities, has played an important role in shaping adult and continuing education, particularly in North America. Besides providing graduate training for many past, current, and future leaders in the field, commission members have helped to shape continuing education literature, have played important leadership roles in national organizations in Canada and the United States, and have helped carry out various annual conferences and workshops on many topics. It is anticipated that although leadership for the field increasingly comes from throughout the world, commission members will continue to play important roles.

A Glimpse into the Future

Previous sections have been designed to provide some argument for the view that continuing educators can and must play important roles in shaping their own destiny. Rather than legislators or funding agencies shaping the field, I believe that a deliberate effort to make desired futures take place must be made by those who practice and study continuing education. Thus, the purpose of this section is to provide a look into the future by examining the effort one institution, Syracuse University, is making to use technological advances in a continuing education program. This future-oriented project, although only completing the first of its initial four years, promises to shape several new directions for the field.

For the past four decades continuing educators at Syracuse University have been collecting a wide variety of print, visual, and media resources related to the education of adults. A large portion of this collection is archival in nature, with the past records of continuing education organizations, associations, and leaders available for historical, bibliographic, and other researchers (Stubblefield, 1980; Hilton, 1985). The collection also contains various material of use to teachers, counselors, and other practitioners. Printed materials alone total nearly 800 linear feet of materials (an estimated three to four million pages), which include correspondence, financial records, published materials, personal papers, photographs, and miscellaneous materials. Thus, the Syracuse University libraries house the most comprehensive assortment of English-language continuing education resources in the world.

Despite the university's commitment to continuing education, storage and processing limitations have made it difficult to make full use of the materials for research purposes or to disseminate those materials to practitioners beyond the Syracuse University campus. The W. K. Kellogg Foundation of Battle Creek, Michigan, has now joined with Syracuse University in an effort to create a continuing education library resource for worldwide use.

Most readers of this sourcebook will know of the tremendous contribution the Kellogg Foundation has made for many years in support of continuing education. Such support has ranged from assisting to build continuing education centers on college campuses initiated in 1951 to more recent efforts aimed at bringing some unity to the field. They have sponsored special retreats for continuing education leaders (Munger, 1985; Smith, 1983); initiated a Kellogg Fellows program to develop new leaders, which graduated its first group in 1983 (Hencey, Arnett, and Lake, 1983); and are now providing large grants to various universities for purposes of developing leadership centers for continuing education and lifelong learning (Long, 1984).

In late 1986 the Kellogg Foundation awarded Syracuse University $3.7 million for an initial four-year project. The university contributed an additional $1.5 million and another $2 million will be raised through endowment efforts over the next several years. The project is designed to develop a system for dissemination of the library resources to continuing educators throughout the world. This project is a useful illustration for this chapter because the latest in electronic transmission, laser technology, optical scanning, and computer storage of information will be used to support dissemination efforts. It is anticipated that numerous developments will take place with implications for the way future continuing educators use information.

There are three major project components. Relative to the first component, the Syracuse University project is developing a full-text information storage, retrieval, and dissemination system based on optical scanning and storage. Optical scanning employs laser technology to rapidly scan and record information in its original form (image data as opposed to the ASCII form now prevalent in computer technology). Materials in the collection will be optically scanned and stored on discs for both massive storage and rapid on-campus retrieval purposes (it may even be possible to digitize the large collection of slides, photographs, and audio-tapes). Computer terminal work stations connected to laser printers will provide users the opportunity to scan large portions of the collection and obtain printed copies of desired original materials. In addition, selected portions of the collection will be made available off campus via such media as CD ROMs (Compact Discs–Read Only Memory). This format will mean that considerable information will be available in one small format, information that can be searched by teachers and learners via a personal computer and special disc drive. Thus, the project is pioneering information storage, retrieval, and dissemination techniques that can be used in a variety of continuing education activities.

This component also is featuring research activities of two types. The first deals with better understanding the history of continuing education as a prelude to better understanding future needs and directions. A specialist in historical research is directing these efforts involving research by on-campus and visiting scholars. The second type of activity involves promoting scholarly activities related to the use of technology in continuing education, including efforts to better understand how information can be disseminated to continuing educators worldwide.

The second component involves developing an interactive communication system. This system involves creating computer software based on a logic-programming language developed at Syracuse University. In information storage and retrieval, the university has long been at the forefront of new knowledge development. The libraries at Syracuse University pioneered the development of on line catalogues, on line text transmission, interactive search capabilities, and high-density storage mechanisms linked to automated access systems. In addition, the Center for Computer Applications and Software Engineering and the School of Computer and Information Science are among the world leaders in developing uses of fifth generation computers and logic programming. Specialists on campus are using these various tools, skills, and experiences to develop software that will powerfully enhance the interactive capability of the information system and enable users to conduct sophisticated research on the collection.

The second project component also involves the development and refinement of an electronic network, AEDNET. AEDNET is designed to link continuing education professionals in various ways. It has the following features:

- A bulletin board service for researchers and practitioners to post research questions, news about professional meetings, and various other types of information
- Electronic mail, message, and text exchange
- Interactive conferencing on questions and problems important to the field

- Access to information about continuing education resources and archival material at Syracuse University
- Special interest groups for electronic information dissemination and sharing
- An electronic journal operated by graduate students in adult education that provides current information about the field.

AEDNET is designed to become a means whereby future continuing educators can have frequent, rapid, and low-cost contact with colleagues throughout the world. (Readers interested in AEDNET should write for information to the Kellogg Project, 113 Euclid, Syracuse University, Syracuse, New York 13244, or email to AEDNET AT SUVM if they have access to BITNET.)

The third component involves facilitation of education related to the dissemination system. One feature of this component is the involvement of a multidisciplinary group of campus scholars who are carefully and systematically investigating the project's potential societal impact. This feature ensures that the attractiveness of new technology does not overshadow the real need to find ways of better disseminating the collection to those who can benefit from it. Thus, professors and graduate students from across the campus are regularly asking difficult questions of project staff and system users, questions that bring attention to important human concerns that must be considered parallel to any technological concerns.

This component also involves special efforts to reach out to continuing educators who might not normally use the collection. International meetings related to the project will be conducted at the conclusion of two, three, and four years. In addition, a distance education graduate program in continuing education is being developed that will enable students from rural North America, developing countries, and other areas to learn about the collection, the continuing education field, and the use of technology to disseminate information to adult students. Throughout the entire project, as a matter of fact, special efforts are being made to provide support to continuing educators from developing countries. One example is the creation of an information counselor work station used by project staff to respond to international queries related to the collection. The information generated will be added to the data base of the project.

Some Future Continuing Education Roles

Technological changes similar to those described in the previous sections, growing professionalization of the field, an ever expanding body of knowledge, and evolving needs of the audiences served are likely to create some new roles for future continuing educators. This section will suggest a few new roles that seem likely to emerge. The role of technology is addressed further by Garrison in Chapter Four.

Information Counseling. This role involves helping adults obtain and use information that they need. The increasing availability of immense amounts of information via electronic data banks means that learners will need assistance in sorting through the possible knowledge bases and search mechanisms. In the future, such a helping role may be done at a distance and with learners from various countries.

Facilitation of Individualized Learning. The rapid improvement of electronic retrieval mechanisms suggests that obtaining information for desired individualized or self-directed learning will become quicker and easier. However, this means that such information will be voluminous and, in many instances, rapidly out of date. Thus, an adult student often will require help from a continuing education specialist in order to know how to organize, prioritize, and use such information effectively and how to efficiently facilitate learning.

Electronic Instruction Specialists. The advance in technology that is fueling the Syracuse University project also is creating both opportunities and challenges related to instruction. Many future continuing educators will need to be skilled in using technology or techniques such as computer-assisted instruction, interactive video, and teleconferencing.

Continuing Education About Electronic Communication. The various advances described above will create a future shock for many adults, in terms of both technological adjustment needs and constant retraining needs. Thus, considerable future continuing education about change, how to adjust to it, and how to cope in terms of new behaviors will be required.

Corresponding Research Related to Technological Change. An important ongoing role for some continuing education scholars is the study of how various technological changes will affect adult learning. Although we are beginning to understand issues related to adult learning, adult development, and cognitive styles, the rapid evolutionary nature of the electronic age will require research, evaluation, and scholarly exchange at a rate much greater than that thus far experienced.

International Facilitators of Development and Information Exchange. The future will no doubt be harder for developing countries than for developed ones. An important, ongoing role for continuing educators in those developed countries must be to assist educators of adults elsewhere in the transition to change, growth in educational expertise, and use of information that will assist in development.

Reflecting on the Future

Regardless of the roles assumed in subsequent years, skill in projecting the future should be helpful, because then it is possible to work toward that future and even create the situations we desire. However, ongoing study to understand both the changes we experience and those we create will always be necessary. This sourcebook provides a useful overview of various topics to think about to prepare for professional work in the year 2000.

References

Bell, D. *Toward the Year 2000: Works in Progress.* Boston: Houghton Mifflin, 1968.

Bell, D. *The Coming of Post-Industrial Society.* New York: Basic Books, 1973.

Bell, W., and Mau, J. A. (eds.). *The Sociology of the Future.* New York: Russell Sage Foundation, 1971.

Cassara, B. B. "The Lifelong Learning Act—An Assessment." *Convergence,* 1979, *12,* 55–63.

Delker, P. V. "Governmental Roles in Lifelong Learning." *Journal of Research and Development in Education,* 1974, 7 (4), 24–33.

Fowles, J. (ed.). *Handbook of Futures Research.* Westport, Conn.: Greenwood Press, 1978.

Glover, R. *Alternative Scenarios of the American Future: 1980–2000.* New York: Future Directions for a Learning Society, College Board, 1979.

Grattan, C. H. *In Quest of Knowledge.* New York: Association Press, 1955.

Gross, R. *The Lifelong Learner.* New York: Simon and Schuster, 1977.

Hanberry, G. C. *Education and Learning for Adults in the 70s and 80s.* College Park: University of Maryland, University College, 1975.

Harrington, F. H. *The Future of Adult Education: New Responsibilities of Colleges and Universities.* San Francisco: Jossey-Bass, 1977.

Healy, G. M. *Toward the Year 2000: Citizens' Ownership of the Future.* Syracuse, N.Y.: Syracuse University, 1979.

Hencey, R., Arnett, J. C., and Lake, K. (eds.). *The Continuity of Change.* Annual Report. Battle Creek, Mich.: W. K. Kellogg Foundation, 1983.

Henley, S. P., and Yates, J. R. *Futurism in Education: Methodology.* Berkeley, Calif.: McCutchan, 1974.

Hiemstra, R. *Lifelong Learning.* Lincoln, Nebr.: Professional Educators Publications, 1976.

Hilton, R. "SUREA: The Grand Canyon of Adult Education Research." *Lifelong Learning: An Omnibus of Practice and Research,* 1985, *8* (7), 16–18, 27.

Himmelstrup, P. "Introduction." In J. Robinson and D. Fielden (eds.), *Strategies for Lifelong Learning.* Esbjerg, Denmark: University Centre of South Jutland, 1980.

Ilsley, P. J. "The Relevance of the Future in Adult Education: A Phenomenological Analysis of Images of the Future." Unpublished doctoral dissertation, Northern Illinois University, 1982.

Jungk, R. *The Everyman Project.* New York: Liveright, 1976.

Kaplan, B. A. *The Future of Citizen Participation in the State of Washington.* Syracuse, N.Y.: Educational Policy Research Center, Syracuse Research Corporation, 1976.

Knowles, M. S. *History of the Adult Education Movement in the United States.* Malabar, Fla.: Robert E. Krieger, 1977.

Long, H. B. (ed.). *Lifelong Learning Forum,* 1984, *1,* 1–3.

Marien, M., and Ziegler, W. L. (eds.). *The Potential of Educational Futures.* Worthington, Ohio: Charles A. Jones, 1972.

Munger, P. D. *Challenges to Higher Education.* Washington, D.C.: Project on Continuing Higher Education Leadership, National University Continuing Education Association, 1985.

Naisbitt, J. *Megatrends*. New York: Warner Books, 1982.

Ohliger, J. "Prospects for a Learning Society." *Adult Leadership,* 1974, *24,* 37–39.

Ross-Macdonald, M., Hassell, M., and McNeill, S. *Life in the Future*. Garden City, N.Y.: Doubleday, 1977.

Roszak, T. *Person/Planet*. Garden City, N.Y.: Anchor Books, 1979.

Smith, W. *Collaboration in Lifelong Learning*. Washington, D.C.: American Association for Adult and Continuing Education, 1983.

Stubblefield, H. W. "An Archive for Adult Education." *Lifelong Learning: The Adult Years,* 1980, *4* (1), 7, 31.

Taylor, R., Rockhill, K., and Fieldhouse, R. *University Adult Education in England and the USA: A Reappraisal of the Liberal Tradition*. Dover, N.H.: Croom-Helm, 1985.

Theobald, R. (ed.). *Futures Conditional*. Indianapolis, Ind.: Bobbs-Merrill, 1972.

Toffler, A. *Future Shock*. New York: Random House, 1970.

Toffler, A. *Learning for Tomorrow: The Role of the Future in Education*. New York: Vintage Books, 1974.

Toffler, A. *The Third Wave*. New York: Bantam Books, 1980.

Verner, C. *Pole's History of Adult Schools*. Washington, D.C.: Adult Education Association of the U.S.A., 1967.

Wagschal, P. H., and Kahn, R. D. (eds.). *Buckminster Fuller on Education*. Amherst: University of Massachusetts Press, 1979.

Ziegler, W. L. (ed.). *Essays on the Future of Continuing Education Worldwide*. Syracuse, N.Y.: Syracuse University Publications in Continuing Education, 1970.

Roger Hiemstra is professor and chair, Adult Education Graduate Program, and director, Kellogg Project, Syracuse University, Syracuse, New York. He is editor, Adult Education Quarterly, *past chair of the Commission of Professors of Adult Education, and has facilitated several futures invention workshops.*

Providers of continuing education must be prepared to make significant adjustments to meet the challenges posed by changing demographic, social, economic, and technological environments.

The Setting for Continuing Education in the Year 2000

Charles H. Fay, Joseph T. McCune, James P. Begin

The need for continuing education in the year 2000 will depend to a great degree on the societal dynamics of the United States and, indeed, world events already in motion. For example, the total number of people in the United States likely to make use of continuing education in 2000 is fixed; all the adults of the year 2000 have already been born. Other factors affecting the demand for continuing education in 2000 are perhaps less fixed, but the forces that will shape the future are operating nonetheless. Without some understanding of these events, continuing education specialists are unlikely to be prepared to meet the needs of the U.S. population as we enter the twenty-first century.

Factors shaping the future of continuing education can be analyzed in terms of trends in six related, but different, areas. The first of these is the nature of the U.S. population. An analysis of demographic trends provides not only an indication of raw numbers of people who will need continuing education in one or more forms but also some idea of the composition of the population as it affects delivery of continuing education.

Second, because continuing education is by nature a follow-up

R. G. Brockett (ed.). *Continuing Education in the Year 2000.*
New Directions for Continuing Education, no. 36. San Francisco: Jossey-Bass, Winter 1987.

activity to basic education, some understanding of the probable nature of traditional education systems at the turn of the century is necessary. Third, understanding what the general U.S. economy will be like in the year 2000 is also necessary, since economic factors are a major determinant both of the need for continuing education and the ability of the society to support it.

Fourth, an examination of technological trends serves a dual purpose. Changes in technology have consistently been a major force in the redesign of jobs and in changing requirements for a usable knowledge and skill base for all adults. At the same time, technological change has allowed delivery of learning systems in new and exciting ways. Much of the impact of technology is mediated by the sociopolitical environment. Thus, government intervention is a fifth major force affecting (supporting and, in some cases, hindering) continuing education efforts in the private and public sectors.

The last area of analysis is trends in organizations and work. While some demand for continuing education will stem from leisure pursuits, the major determinant will be needs arising from changing work demands on the population. As the nature of work changes, employees will have to renew and replace skills. Organizations themselves will change in response to the other factors we are discussing, such as the new economic and technological pressures. Thus, their demand for labor will change.

It is worthwhile noting at this point that forecasting the future, even a future so near as the year 2000, is a risky business, and forecasts depend to some extent on the degree to which the forecaster is an optimist or a pessimist. Some of the futurist writers prophesy war and pestilence (Lamm, 1985), while others predict everything "coming up roses" (*The New American Boom*, 1986). In fact, the future probably lies in between, and that position is the one taken in this chapter. Regardless of the optimism level of the prophet, it is worthwhile, as noted by the Carnegie Council on Policy Studies in Higher Education (1980), to make those predictions: "Looking ahead is a risky endeavor. Speculations about the future, however, can be useful. They can encourage others . . . to think about what is already largely determined . . . , about what is likely but not certain to change . . . , about what might happen, both for the better and worse, that is now unknown . . . , about the tools at hand . . . , and think about how individual institutions may react to these developments and possibilities" (p. 15).

Demographic Trends

The U.S. population likely to need continuing education in the year 2000 is, as noted above, already alive today. In 1984 the total population of the United States was around 237 million. In 1995 it is estimated that total population will grow to about 260 million; estimates for the year 2000 vary, but the total population at that time is likely to be around 270 million. Population increase has slowed; in the 1980s it has been averaging around 1.2 percent per year, while only a 0.8 percent increase is forecast for the 1990s (U.S. Department of Labor, 1986).

In addition to total population, the supply and type of workers is determined by the basic age distribution, family structure, mortality and morbidity patterns, immigration, role of minorities in society, and geographic shifts (Bezold, Carlson, and Peck, 1986). As an example, the age distribution of the population is changing, with the median age rising from 30.6 in 1982 to 36.3 in 2000 (Cetron, Soriano, and Gayle, 1985). Even though the total population is increasing, some segments are decreasing in absolute numbers, as well as relative to the population as a whole. The U.S. population of prime work age (30 to 59) will have the largest increase over the period, and the population aged under 18 and over 70 will also increase. The population between 19 and 29 and between 60 and 69 will decrease (U.S. Department of Labor, 1986).

A continued change in family structure can be expected along the line currently seen. That is, the traditional U.S. family, with working father, homemaker mother, and children, will be increasingly supplanted by single-parent families, individuals living in a variety of sharing arrangements, and dual-career couples (Bezold, Carlson, and Peck, 1986). This will result in higher labor force participation rates of women, and, in fact, much of the increase in the labor force is projected on the basis of increased participation by women.

Mortality and morbidity patterns are expected to change substantially, affecting both how long we live and how long we are able to work. Demographers refer to the "squaring of the survival curve" (Bezold, Carlson, and Peck, 1986). Plotted age distributions have traditionally looked like triangles, with gaps on the male side produced by wars. Increasingly a plot of age distributions will look like a rectangle, with most individuals living longer. In addition, morbidity or ill health of the sort that prevents labor force participation is likely to be postponed until the last few years of life.

The role of minorities will be even greater in the year 2000 than it is now. Minorities are expected to compose 29 percent of the population by the year 2000. If immigration patterns and differential birth rates persist, whites may become a minority in the country by the end of the twenty-first century (Cetron, Soriano, and Gayle, 1985; Bezold, Carlson, and Peck, 1986). The makeup of minorities is shifting as well. Hispanics will supplant blacks as the largest minority by 2000 (Bezold, Carlson, and Peck, 1986). Thus, a larger portion of the U.S. population entering the work force may speak English only as a second language.

Population increases will vary by region, and the increase will vary by age in these regions. On the whole, the population will continue to shift toward the South (up by 31 percent between 1980 and 2000) and the West (up by 45 percent in the same period), while declining in the Midwest (down by 1 percent between 1990 and 2000) and the Northeast (down by 6 percent in the same period). The Northeast will have an overbalance of older adults, while the West will have a heavier concentration of younger people; the Midwest and South will be similar to national distributions (U.S. Department of Labor, 1986). Within regions, the trend of movement away from central cities to suburbs, nonmetropolitan areas, and rural areas seems irreversible (Choate, 1984).

Trends in labor force participation are similar to trends in the total population, although on a smaller scale: In 1985 there was a 65.9 percent participation rate, with a total labor force of 118.6 million. By 2000 the participation rate will be slightly larger, at 68 percent, resulting in a total labor force of 137.8 million (Bezold, Carlson, and Peck, 1986). The trend toward slightly earlier retirement is expected to continue. Trends in participation by race and gender have changed significantly in recent years, and those changes are expected to continue. While participation by race is not expected to change in terms of percentage participation, the distribution of minorities in many job categories will increase.

Finally, educational levels are expected to increase. In 1970 about 13 percent of the labor force between the ages of eighteen and sixty-four had four or more years of college. By 1984, 22 percent had four or more years of college, and nearly half the labor force had one or more years of college (U.S. Department of Labor, 1986). By the year 2000 much more of the labor force will possess a college degree.

To summarize, the work force will be significantly different from that of today. Its makeup will more nearly reflect the underlying population in terms of gender and race. Overall, it will be a better-educated and older work force, one capable of continuing work well into what we now consider old age. New family patterns will make working into later years necessary. A shortage of young workers will require organizations to rely more on these older workers, whose skills are likely to become obsolete. The implications of these demographic trends will be made evident throughout the following discussion.

Traditional Educational Trends

The structure of educational organizations is likely to change substantially by 2000. Driven by a need to use resources more efficiently, public schools are likely to offer a wider variety of educational service to a broader client base. Thus, by 2000 schools may be open twenty-four hours a day, twelve months a year, providing educational service to traditional students, the business community, and other parts of the community (Cetron, Soriano, and Gayle, 1985).

Educational services to traditional students are likely to change in intensity and nature. Children are likely to enter the school system at age three, and most students can, at a minimum, expect to be involved in educational activities a minimum of seven hours a day for 210 days per year. Older students will be exposed to a wider variety of programs than are currently available, largely due to the availability of interactive computer/video technology, and may work with master teachers, serve in apprenticeship programs, and spend more time in labs, music classes, vocational education classes, and individual and group tutoring sessions. Because much of the rote learning tasks can be handled by interactive computer technology, teachers will have more time to spend on mentoring tasks (Cetron, Soriano, and Gayle, 1985).

Colleges may increasingly be the base for older students, with graduate-level courses taught to more experienced undergraduates. All schools will be likely to generate income by providing training and retraining services to business, because schools will see the training and retraining market as a means of generating income through otherwise unused resources, thus lowering tax rates for traditional educational services. Because changing technologies require a more educated work force, and one that can be more readily retrained, businesses are already forming partnerships with schools in many locales and are likely to support schools moving into the provision of training and retraining to business (Cetron, Soriano, and Gayle, 1985).

Economic Trends

A number of trends shaping the economy of 2000 have been noted. The most important of these is the rise of the service and information economy. Other trends contributing to greater competition and a more unstable environment include the globalization of the economy, a possible decline (one relatively accepted form of economic forecast, the Kondratieff Wave projection, predicts an economic low point, or trough, near 2000), increased entrepreneurial activity, the elimination of intermediaries (such as wholesalers) as economic agents, and the growth of the informal economy (such as bartering and illegal activities) to become as much as 50 percent of total economic activity (Bezold, Carlson, and Peck, 1986).

However, the economic picture is seen optimistically by most, with projections for a steadily rising gross national product, inflation under control, unemployment at low levels, and increasing productivity (Gallup and Proctor, 1984). This does not mean that getting from here to there will be automatic or without economic dislocations for many people, but many economists believe that with proper management the prospects are positive.

Technological change will drive the economy as it changes from a goods and services economy to a services and information economy. The pace of technological change and the impact of international competition will result in frequent changes in jobs for most workers, making retraining a necessity (Choate, 1984). By the year 2000, as many as 80 percent of all workers in the United States will be employed in the information industry (Feingold, 1984). This will have a major impact on workers as economic units. In an industrial age, workers are expendable cogs in the machine; in an information age (and to a lesser extent, in a service age), human capital is the most valuable capital an organization has (Russel, 1986). To protect this capital, organizations will have to invest heavily in retraining.

Technological Trends

Technological change has already reduced the number of manufacturing workers needed by U.S. industry through automation and has rendered the skills of thousands of workers obsolete through increasingly "de-skilling" manufacturing processes. This can be witnessed as we see shorter product life cycles (a phenomenon particularly emphasized by the Japanese) and the emergent new products requiring employee skills very different from those used by producing the old product.

Advances in technology by the year 2000 will cause greater turmoil in society and in the workplace than any other factor. On the one hand, it is estimated that robotics technology might displace forty to fifty million U.S. workers from their jobs by 2000 (Bezold, Carlson, and Peck, 1986). Other forecasters are less pessimistic; they project job displacement at closer to three million (Feingold, 1984). Under any circumstances, the advent and development of new electronic, information, and communication technologies will create millions of new jobs at the same time as they cause the disappearance of old professions and specializations (Ferrarotti, 1986). These new jobs will require more knowledge and decision-making abilities from workers; thus the faster the pace of technological change, the greater the need for worker retraining (Watts, 1984).

If technological changes will force frequent retraining, they will also make that retraining more feasible and more effective. The driving technologies of the information economy are the electronic memory, voice processing, expert systems, and networking (Russel, 1986). These are also the technologies that can improve educational delivery systems.

AT&T, for example, has proposed an education utility that takes advantage of these technologies to make educational opportunity as common as electric power—a utility service (Gooler, 1986). Individuals could hook into the utility at home, in formal classrooms, at work, or anywhere educational resources were needed. Its proposers see the utility as providing community educational services (such as educational bulletin boards, adult basic education, health information, and parent education programs), elective continued learning, vocational career preparation (including interactive assessment of interests and abilities, information on career options and requirements, and direct vocational education), and continuing professional education, as well as a delivery system for corporate training. The future role of technology in continuing education is addressed further by Garrison in Chapter Four.

Sociopolitical Trends

Economic dislocations have already done much to reduce the loyalty of workers, and even manager-workers, to organizations. Unions have not been very successful in protecting jobs for their members. There has been increased emphasis on the legal rights of individual workers, so that the doctrine of "at will" employment has been eroded in the private sector. In fact, legislation regulating plant closings has been adopted by four states and is pending in thirteen others (Harrison, 1984). So far, however, neither union nor government has been able to protect workers from economic displacement. However, both institutions have seen retraining as a major cushion for displaced workers, and that emphasis is likely to grow as the information economy develops. A tighter linkage between private sector labor skills needs and government retraining expenditures has been taking place, as indicated by the use of private industry councils under the Jobs Training Partnership Act (JTPA) to determine training needs. This linkage should increase by 2000 and may help establish retraining rights as a middle ground between unregulated layoffs and job tenure.

For those workers who are not threatened by displacement, survival and standard of living are likely to be taken for granted, and more emphasis will be placed on personal growth and self-development as a motive for working; for those with reduced working opportunities, the primary focus will shift outside the workplace (Yankelovich and Immerwahr, 1984). Value shifts in the population include a greater concern for creativity and autonomy, a rejection of authority, the placement of self-expression over status, an emphasis on pleasure seeking coupled with a hunger for new experiences, a quest for community, a demand for participation in decision making, a desire for adventure, and a need for self-cultivation and inner growth (Bezold, Carlson, and Peck, 1986).

Organizational and Work Trends

Work organizations have changed considerably from the single product, regional market firms of the early 1800s. Since then, organizational forms have evolved from individually controlled agencies emphasizing a single product within a local or regional market to a complex organizational structure emphasizing standard and innovative products in both stable and changing markets. Between now and 2000 the continuing education needs of business will shift from functional and limited general management training to an emphasis on general management and high-level functional education (Miles, 1985).

The need to remain competitive in increasingly competitive times has forced many organizations to cut operating costs. Because payroll is often the organization's largest single expenditure, it is frequently the first (and often the only) area to be cut. In addition, mergers, takeovers (whether friendly or hostile), and other corporate restructurings often result in the layoff of employees. This trend will continue as the new economy of 2000 affects organizations and the nature of work itself. Organizations in established sectors of the economy are likely to continue consolidation but become more efficient by flattening organizational structures, automating to the extent possible, and making appropriate investments in human capital (Klaus, 1984).

Current estimates for formal and informal employee training expenditures by organizations exceed $210 billion (compared with elementary and secondary education expenditures of $144 billion, and postsecondary education expenditures of $94 billion). The forecast of a substantial growth in need for training suggests that organizations will need to spend immense amounts (*Serving the New Corporation*, 1986), with one estimate of corporate outlays for training exceeding 10 percent of payroll by the mid 1990s (*The New American Boom*, 1986).

Jobs in the new organizations will be different. Most workers' jobs will change dramatically every five to ten years, so that most workers will be displaced frequently and will move not only from one job to another but even from one occupation to another (Cetron, Soriano, and Gayle, 1985). The workweek will continue to shrink to around twenty-five to thirty hours by 2000, and more people will work at home (Bezold, Carlson, and Peck, 1986). It has been estimated that approximately 450 companies already have formal and informal telecommuting programs, involving over 100,000 employees working at computer terminals either at home or in remote locations (Larson, 1985). This home work will increase because of the new technologies, and it is desirable because it fits in with new family patterns (such as more single-parent families), worker concerns for independence and autonomy, and organizational efforts to trim budgets and remain flexible by subcontracting rather than hiring human capital.

More work will lend itself to subcontracting in the information economy, since much routine work will be automated, and the value of many workers will lie in their ability to handle discretionary tasks. The new worker is one who has increased knowledge and decision-making abilities, but even more, one who is capable of frequent and rapid shifts in job duties and assignments.

The Setting for Continuing Education in the Year 2000

Need. Barring the gloomier predictions of war and pestilence, it is virtually certain that the need for continuing education will be even greater in the year 2000 than it is today. Shifts in the economy and increasingly rapid changes in technology will result in jobs that change radically every five to ten years. At the same time, demographic shifts will be bringing large numbers of nontraditional workers into the economy who may be less prepared to deal with short-cycle change. Similarly, since workers will be staying in the labor force longer, they will be faced with a larger number of changes in their work span.

The needs of organizations will increasingly focus on the retrainable employee who can cope with frequent change. Because more work will be subcontracted to individual home workers, who are less likely to live in central cities, traditional corporate in-plant training methods are not the answer for many retraining needs.

Supply. If technology is creating the need for increased training efforts, it is also making these efforts more feasible. The very information economy that will cause dislocation is also the economy that can make the shift a humane one. The combination of interactive computing, communications networks, video technology, expert systems, and related technologies makes possible the kind of educational utility noted above or smaller, more specialized networks.

Suppliers of traditional education will be facing a stagnant market in terms of school-age children at the same time that the introduction of improved technologies will greatly increase educational system productivity. It seems probable that these suppliers will seek to make more efficient use of their resources by becoming major suppliers of continuing education and retraining.

New competitors will appear in the area of continuing education as well. A number of private companies are offering traditional degrees that have been accredited by the appropriate accreditation bodies: McDonald's Hamburger University offers an A.A.S., for example (Nadler and Wiggs, 1986). Arthur D. Little Management Education Institute offers an M.S.; Bell and Howell's De Vry Institute of Technology, a B.A. and an A.A.S.; the Wang Institute of Graduate Studies, an M.S.; and the Rand Graduate Institute, a Ph.D. As traditional education institutions, both secondary and postsecondary, move toward providing continuing education for workers in conjunction with their employers, other nontraditional groups, less constrained by traditional educational institution cultures, will pose increasing competition.

Implications for Providers of Continuing Education

Guest (1986) has proposed that management imperatives for the year 2000 will include fully utilizing the skills and motivational potential of employees and helping employees and managers adapt to the changes in their work lives brought about by the organization's continually evolving internal and external environments. If they are to address these future concerns effectively, continuing education providers must act more as partners with their end-users rather than just as vendors. Providers must continually modify their programs to ensure that training programs offered are consistent with the changing needs of end-users. Developing long-term relationships with users will enable providers to advise organizations of ways to prepare employees for future changes.

Entirely new methods of continuing education may need to be developed to respond to employees' changing educational needs. The action research model may provide a useful framework for continuing education providers of the future (French and Bell, 1984). This approach combines a concern for procedural justice with a focus on the application of research findings to specific organizational problems. Thus, research leads to action that leads to more research, and it does so in a context in which there is a concern for the needs of the employee as well as the needs of the organization.

An important concern of future trainers will involve helping employees adapt to changes at work. Recent research has begun to focus on problems related to career transitions (Brett, 1984; Latack and Dozier, 1986). Researchers have developed a model of career transitions that describes how an individual makes sense of a change in work roles (Louis, 1980). This process model consists of the following phases: (1) comparing the new role with the old role by determining the contrasts, changes, and surprises; (2) interpreting these differences in light of past experiences, personality, and personal cognitive map; (3) attributing meaning to these differences; and (4) selecting a behavioral response, revising the cognitive map, and changing anticipations.

Such models appear useful in designing education and training programs to facilitate successful work transitions. They would also be useful in guiding organizational policies with respect to employee transition actions. The dissemination and development of career and work transition research, along with the development of specific training programs sensitive to research findings, will be a major challenge and responsibility for providers of continuing education if they are to meet the challenges of the year 2000.

One recent example of this approach involved the burnout problem found among some groups of professionals such as social workers (Cherniss, 1980). Researchers were able to identify the causes of the problem (that is, characteristics of the work), and programs were developed to train managers and professionals in ways of handling and preventing burnout in their organizations. This model of continuing education will become even more important as the trends discussed in this chapter begin to affect U.S. organizations.

Other innovative instructional methods will likely include a variety of sabbatical programs for managers. Miles (1985) foresees the establishment of midcareer centers serving executives and their families, with access to many programs of major universities.

In summary, as we approach the next century, providers of continuing education will face increasingly difficult challenges and problems. They have the opportunity to make a major impact on the effective functioning of organizations by increasing the adaptability and effectiveness of employees. Perhaps more important, providers of continuing education have the opportunity to make the inevitable process of change a much more humane one.

References

Bezold, C., Carlson, R. J., and Peck, J. C. *The Future of Work and Health*. Dover, Mass.: Auburn House, 1986.

Brett, J. "Job Transitions and Personal and Role Development." In K. Rowland and G. R. Ferris (eds.), *Research in Personnel and Human Resource Management*. Vol. 2. Greenwich, Conn.: Jai Press, 1984.

Carnegie Council on Policy Studies in Higher Education. *Three Thousand Futures: The Next Twenty Years for Higher Education*. San Francisco: Jossey-Bass, 1980.

Cetron, M. J., Soriano, B., and Gayle, B. *Schools of the Future: How American Business and Education Can Cooperate to Save Our Schools*. New York: McGraw-Hill, 1985.

Cherniss, C. *Staff Burnout: Job Stress in the Human Services*. Newbury Park, Calif.: Sage, 1980.

Choate, P. "Employers Will Follow Workers South and West . . . " In *Work in the 21st Century*. New York: Hippocrene Books, 1984.

Feingold, S. N. "Tracking New Career Categories . . . " In *Work in the 21st Century*. New York: Hippocrene Books, 1984.

Ferrarotti, F. *Five Scenarios for the Year 2000*. New York: Greenwood Press, 1986.

French, W. L., and Bell, C. H., Jr. *Organizational Development: Behavioral Science Interventions for Organizational Improvements*. Englewood Cliffs, N.J.: Prentice-Hall, 1984.

Gallup, G., Jr., and Proctor, W. *Forecast 2000*. New York: William Morrow, 1984.

Gooler, D. D. *The Education Utility: The Power to Revitalize Education and Society*. Englewood Cliffs, N.J.: Educational Technology Publications, 1986.

Guest, R. H. "Management Imperatives for the Year 2000." *California Management Review*, 1986, *23*, 62–70.

Harrison, J. B. "Comparing European and American Experience with Plant Closing Laws." In B. D. Dennis (ed.), *Proceedings of the Thirty-Sixth Annual Meeting*. Madison, Wisc.: Industrial Relations Research Association, 1984.

Klaus, G. "Corporate Pyramids Will Tumble . . . ." In *Work in the 21st Century*. New York: Hippocrene Books, 1984.

Lamm, R. D. *Megatraumas: America at the Year 2000*. Boston: Houghton Mifflin, 1985.

Larson, E. "Working at Home: Is It Freedom or a Life of Flabby Loneliness?" *Wall Street Journal*, Feb. 13, 1985, 33.

Latack, J. C., and Dozier, J. B. "After the Ax Falls: Job Loss or a Career Transition." *Academy of Management Review*, 1986, *11*, 375–392.

Louis, M. R. "Career Transitions: Varieties and Commonalities." *Academy of Management Review*, 1980, *5*, 329–340.

Miles, R. E. "The Future of Business Education." *California Management Review*, 1985, *22*, 63–73.

Nadler, L., and Wiggs, G. D. *Managing Human Resource Development: A Practical Guide*. San Francisco: Jossey-Bass, 1986.

The New American Boom. Washington, D.C.: Kiplinger Washington Editors, 1986.

Russel, R. A. *Winning the Future*. New York: Carroll & Graf, 1986.

Serving the New Corporation. Alexandria, Va.: American Society for Training and Development, 1986.

U.S. Department of Labor, Bureau of Labor Statistics. *Occupational Projections and Training Data*. U.S. Bureau of Labor Statistics Bulletin 2251. Washington, D.C.: U.S. Government Printing Office, 1986.

Watts, G. "Training and Retraining Workers Will Be an Important Challenge . . .-" In *Work in the 21st Century*. New York: Hippocrene Books, 1984.

Yankelovich, D., and Immerwahr, J. "The Emergence of Expressiveness . . . " In *Work in the 21st Century*. New York: Hippocrene Books, 1984.

Charles H. Fay is assistant professor of industrial relations and human resources at the Institute of Management and Labor Relations, Rutgers University. He has developed and taught continuing education courses in performance management, compensation, human resource information systems, and other management areas for the Management Development Center at the institute. He is also an instructor in the American Compensation Association's Certification Program.

Joseph T. McCune is assistant professor of industrial relations and human resources at the Institute of Management and Labor Relations, Rutgers University. He developed and administers the Human Resource Management Certificate Program for the Management Development Center at the institute, and teaches training and development, job analysis, and other courses in that program. He helped originate a segment on organizational development and change for the Certified Public Manager Program for the State of New Jersey.

James P. Begin is professor of industrial relations and human resources and director, Institute of Management and Labor Relations, Rutgers University. He has been on the faculty at Rutgers since 1969 when he received his doctorate from Purdue University. As director, his responsibilities include a range of continuing education programs that enroll approximately 12,000 students a year.

Recent developments in research have increased understanding of the adult learner and provide direction for future investigation.

Trends in Research on the Adult Learner

Ralph G. Brockett, Gordon G. Darkenwald

Historically, the field of continuing education has emphasized practice over theory and research. Yet, a body of professional literature has continued to evolve over the past several decades, and much of this literature has focused on providing a greater understanding of the adult learner. In particular, the past thirty years or so have witnessed much growth in the research-based literature related to adult learning and the adult learner. Future practice in continuing education has the potential to be informed by research in a way that has previously not been possible, due to lack of this research base.

Research on adult learning and the adult learner can be traced to Thorndike's (1928) seminal study, which provided perhaps the earliest evidence to dispel the myth that adult learning ability declines steadily with age and paved the way for a branch of research that remains active today. In the early 1950s, Essert observed that the field was in the process of "drawing the broad outlines of a program of more substantive research" (1953, p. 198). Similarly, Houle (1953) suggested that the full potential of continuing education "can only be realized if the work in this field is guided by intelligent, mature, and disciplined thought" (p. 273). Several years, later, Brunner and his colleagues (Brunner, Wilder, Kirchner, and Newberry, 1959) published their extensive review, which

R. G. Brockett (ed.). *Continuing Education in the Year 2000.*
New Directions for Continuing Education, no. 36. San Francisco: Jossey-Bass, Winter 1987.

included numerous suggestions for future research. More recently, Long (1983) reviewed current research on several major topics and concluded that although many of the problems identified by earlier scholars have not been resolved, the picture for the future is encouraging. Indeed, there is evidence to support the view that an increased emphasis on research can be seen in the literature of the field (Dickinson and Rusnell, 1971; Long, 1977).

A criticism of much adult learning research to date has been the disjointed or scattered nature of such efforts. This concern was raised by Brunner and his associates (Brunner, Wilder, Kirchner, and Newberry, 1959) and remains relevant today (Darkenwald and Merriam, 1982). Beder (1985), for instance, recently observed that with the exception of two areas, participation and self-directed learning, research-based knowledge of continuing education remains limited.

We believe that a key to building a solid future knowledge base on adult learning is to be found in sustained efforts to pursue inquiry on topics relevant to the broad field of continuing education. The shotgun approach that has characterized much of the research in continuing education will need to be replaced with an active effort to build long-term agendas in key areas. In order to initiate these agendas, it is logical to begin building on some of the areas that have been or are emerging currently as important research themes.

In this chapter, it is our intent to explore likely directions for the future of adult learning research. To do this, we begin by describing three current research areas we believe will serve as a foundation for future efforts: the teaching-learning transaction, participation, and self-directed learning. We will then consider several factors likely to be important in improving and expanding future research. While research in continuing education will continue on topics other than learning, we have limited our focus to the adult learner, since this area has direct relevance to improving practice in the delivery of educational experiences.

Teaching-Learning Transaction

Most research in adult learning to date has emphasized the role of the learner. The role of the teacher or facilitator has been given secondary attention. At the same time, there is evidence that the teacher of adults can make a difference. Several recent books, for instance, stress the importance of the facilitator in the process of adult learning (Brookfield, 1986; Knox, 1986; Daloz, 1986). Thus, the teaching-learning transaction seems worthy of a closer look in terms of its potential as a future research direction. Three aspects of the research in this area are considered below.

Teaching Adults and Children. A major assumption that Knowles (1980) makes in his model of andragogy is that in order to create an ideal learning situation, there need to be differences in how adults and children are taught. Do such differences exist in practice? To answer this question, Beder and Darkenwald (1982) administered a questionnaire to 173 teachers in public school and college settings who taught both adults and pre-adults (children and adolescents). They found that these teachers did, indeed, report differences in how they teach the different groups. With adults, the teachers reported using more variety in their teaching techniques, making use of the learners' experiences in the classroom context, and being more responsive to learners' feedback about content. On the other hand, with pre-adults, the same teachers reported they emphasized a greater degree of structure and spent more time giving directions, dealing with discipline issues, and offering emotional support to individual students. The authors concluded that "teachers do in fact teach adults differently from children" and that "adults are perceived as more motivated, pragmatic, self-directed, and task-oriented than pre-adults" (p. 142).

In a follow-up factor analysis of the data from this study, an effort was made to determine if the reported differences reflected some sort of underlying conceptual structure (Darkenwald, 1982). Two factors were identified as comprising this conceptual structure: (1) control and structure of the teaching-learning transaction and (2) flexibility and responsiveness to learners. It was concluded that tentative support exists for the view that "teachers tended to be more learner-centered or responsive and less controlling or teacher-centered when teaching adults" (p. 203) as opposed to pre-adults.

The above studies are based on self-reported behavior of teachers. Building on these findings, Gorham (1985) was interested in determining the extent to which reported behaviors were consistent with observed behaviors in the classroom. She administered a slightly modified version of the questionnaire mentioned above to 115 teachers. Then, using a systematic technique for objectively describing classroom teaching behavior, she was able to compare reported and actual instructional behaviors. Gorham found that while teachers reported differences in how they taught adults and pre-adults, there were no observed differences in how the two age groups were taught.

Measuring Teaching Styles. The studies described above provide evidence that most teachers believe there are differences in how different age groups should be taught and that there may be inconsistencies between what many teachers believe and what they practice. A direction for future research might revolve around the issue of appropriate teaching approaches and potential discrepancies between beliefs and actions. Two instruments have recently been developed that may prove valuable in the exploration of these questions. One of these, the Philosophy of Adult Education Inventory (PAEI) (Zinn, 1983), is a scale that describes the extent to which one subscribes to underlying principles of liberal, progressive, behaviorist, humanist, and radical philosophies of continuing education as described by Elias and Merriam (1980). By understanding the philosophical orientations of those who teach adults, it should be possible to better understand major assumptions underlying practice.

A second instrument that holds promise for future efforts to study the teaching-learning transaction is the Principles of Adult Learning Scale (PALS) (Conti, 1985a, 1985b). PALS is a forty-four–item Likert scale designed to assess the degree to which teachers subscribe to principles of teaching adults as reflected in the predominant literature of the field. Conti suggests that teaching style can be viewed as a continuum, with a collaborative teaching style, characterized by progressive, learner-centered behaviors, at one extreme and a teacher-directed style, with an emphasis on low responsiveness and traditional or teacher-centered behaviors, at the other extreme. Thus, PALS can be used to measure the basic beliefs that teachers of adults hold. It should have value in building a knowledge base related to understanding the role of the facilitator and the beliefs that influence this role. The PAEI and PALS each hold much promise for the future, both as research instruments and as diagnostic tools for use by continuing education practitioners.

Classroom Social Environment Research. Until recently, inquiry regarding the components and effects of the classroom social environment or climate has been confined to school settings. The focus of this line of research is the classroom, or other organized educational format, conceived as a "dynamic social system that includes not only teacher behavior, and teacher-student interaction but also student-student interaction" (Moos, 1979, p. 138). Numerous studies in schools have demonstrated that classroom social climate exerts potent effects on such student outcomes as achievement, attendance, and satisfaction. Thus, research in this area holds much promise for the improvement of practice.

In a study by Darkenwald and Gavin (1987), Moos's widely employed Classroom Environment Scale (CES), a measure of high school classroom social environment, was used to predict dropout from teacher-centered high school equivalency classes. Only one of seven CES subscales was associated with dropout. The authors concluded that the CES was inappropriate for assessing adult class environments, noting the need for an adult version of the CES or a totally new instrument.

Subsequently, a new instrument, the Adult Classroom Environment Scale (ACES), was developed. Three forms of ACES were produced: Student Ideal, Student Actual, and Teacher Actual. The term *actual* refers to perceptions of the real or enacted environment. The forms are identical except for some differences in tense and directions to respondents, thus permitting cross-form comparisons (Darkenwald, 1987a).

Briefly, the exploratory findings revealed discrepancies between student and teacher perceptions in three very different adult education settings. In general, scale scores followed a hierarchical pattern, with Student Ideal highest, Teacher Actual next, and Student Actual lowest. Since ACES was designed to describe a positive, growth-enhancing adult learning environment, these discrepancies indicate cause for concern. Several studies using the Adult Classroom Environment Scale are currently in progress and should contribute significantly to the cumulative development of tested knowledge in this area.

Participation

Because adults generally engage in organized educational activities voluntarily, participation behavior has been, and will continue to be, a major focus for research in continuing education. The body of research on participation, most of it consisting of descriptive surveys, is enormous. In the following pages, it is possible only to note briefly some current trends that seem promising for the future development of tested knowledge and theory. Comprehensive discussions of the general literature can be found in Cross (1981), Darkenwald and Merriam (1982), Long (1983), and Scanlan (1986).

Life Transitions. The importance of change events, such as getting a new job, becoming a parent, or losing a spouse through death or divorce, in influencing participation behavior was discussed by Knox (1977) a decade ago. A large-scale survey by Aslanian and Brickell (1980) found that such life transitions, which they termed trigger events, were major precipitating factors in adults' decisions to enroll. The pragmatic implication is for continuing educators to capitalize on these teachable moments.

Shortcomings in the Aslanian and Brickell study, specifically a disproportionately middle-class sample and certain leading questions, raise the issue of whether or not their findings correctly estimate the salience of change events or life transitions. Replications are needed, as well as cross-cultural research, to further develop this promising line of inquiry. Moreover, future researchers should employ more sophisticated analytical tools to address dimensions of the life transition and participation phenomenon requiring advanced statistical methods. There is also a need for naturalistic inquiries on the relationship between life transitions and change events and engagement in both organized and self-directed education. Without such a grounded, phenomenological knowledge base, quantitative researchers may ask many of the wrong questions.

Psychosocial Factors. A scattering of studies on the relationships between certain psychological and psychosocial variables, such as locus of control, anomie, and reference group influences, suggest some promising directions for future research. Perhaps the studies of anomie have yielded the best-developed line of inquiry in this general area.

Research on different populations (Fisher, 1979; Garry, 1977) indicates that adults with high levels of anomie seldom participate in continuing education. Moreover, in Garry's study, high levels of anomie were negatively associated not only with participation but with positive attitudes toward continuing education. Attitudes, as Scanlan (1986) suggests, are probably among the most potent predictors of participation. Until recently, no valid and reliable attitude measure had been constructed. This gap has been remedied (Darkenwald and Hayes, in press). The new instrument should make a contribution to inquiries on the relationships of attitudes not only to participation but also to other participation-related variables.

For research exploring the effects on participation of reference groups, see especially Murphy (1977) and Gooderham (1987). Findings of these and other studies suggest that this variable has a significant independent effect on participation behavior.

Deterrents to Participation. Although descriptive surveys have invariably queried respondents about "barriers to participation," rigorous analyses of deterrents to participation have appeared in the literature only recently. Deterrents research has obvious practical utility for program planning and marketing. Equally important is the potential contribution to theory building of the developing body of knowledge on deterrents to participation. Every major theory of participation behavior (Cross, 1981; Darkenwald and Merriam, 1982; Rubenson, 1977) identifies deterrents, or barriers, as a major explanatory construct. Until recently, however, no valid and reliable measures of this construct existed.

The void in instrumentation and substantive findings began to be remedied in 1984 with the development of a factor-analyzed scale to assess barriers to participation in health-related continuing education (Scanlan and Darkenwald, 1984). This instrument succeeded in accounting for 40 percent of the variance in participation status, as opposed to the usual 10 percent or so. In 1985 a new scale to measure deterrents to participation among the general public was published, along with substantive findings based on factor analytic and correlational procedures (Darkenwald and Valentine, 1985). These large-sample factor analyses revealed that earlier, intuitive conceptualizations of barriers to participation (for example, Cross, 1981) were invalid. Moreover, it has been established that the deterrents construct is multidimensional and varies in structure for different subgroups of the adult population. Cross-cultural studies of deterrents are currently under way, and a typology of subgroups of deterred adults, based on cluster analysis, is forthcoming (Darkenwald and Valentine, in press).

Although this line of inquiry is developing rapidly, much more work needs to be done in the years ahead before research on deterrents realizes its full potential for the improvement of professional practice.

Self-Directed Learning

With the growth of nontraditional opportunities for adult learners, it is becoming increasingly important to better understand the adult who opts to assume primary responsibility for planning, implementing, and evaluating his or her own learning. Thus, a third area likely to have implications for future research revolves around the phenomenon of self-directed learning. The knowledge base of self-directed learning has exploded since the initial publication of Tough's (1971) findings on the learning projects of adults. In this study, Tough interviewed sixty-six adults about the frequency and nature of their major learning efforts during the course of a year. He found that when the definition of learning is expanded to include activities taking place outside the classroom setting, most adults engage in a wide range of activities, the vast majority of which are planned, implemented, and evaluated primarily by the learners themselves. During the years following Tough's study, numerous replications basically supported the findings of the initial study. Today, it is estimated that at least 70 percent of all learning activities in which adults engage are primarily self-planned.

As evidence to support the predominance of self-planning in adult learning grew, researchers began to look toward questions addressing the characteristics of self-directedness and the process of facilitating self-directed learning. One approach has been to use qualitative research methods to understand self-directed learning from the perspective of the learners themselves. These approaches, which have included interviews, case studies, and content analysis, have made a contribution to the theoretical underpinnings of self-directed learning and hold promise for addressing many of the questions that could contribute to further understanding of learner self-direction (Brockett, 1985b).

Still another approach to studying self-directed learning has been made possible through the development of instruments designed to measure learners' levels of self-directedness. Two instruments developed to date are the Self-Directed Learning Readiness Scale (SDLRS) and the Oddi Continuing Learning Inventory (OCLI). The SDLRS (Guglielmino, 1977) is a fifty-eight–item Likert scale designed to measure the degree to which individuals perceive themselves to possess skills and attitudes frequently associated with self-directed learning. Studies using this instrument have found support for relationships between self-directedness and such characteristics as creativity, positive self-concept, life satisfaction, health-promoting behavior, and motivational orientations (Brockett, 1985b). Similarly, the OCLI is a twenty-four–item Likert scale that "describes personality characteristics of self-directed continuing learners" (Oddi, 1986, p. 97). Using this instrument, Shaw (1987) reported a positive relationship between self-directedness and intellectual development among college students between the ages of seventeen and fifty-four. However, Six and Hiemstra (1987) found that the OCLI was not a predictive measure of self-directedness in the classroom setting. While both the SDLRS and the OCLI have made important contributions to our understanding of self-directedness, their possible limitations (Brockett, 1985a; Six and Hiemstra, 1987) suggest that it is important to clearly understand the parameters of these scales in order to avoid potential misuse.

Clearly, self-directed learning research has mushroomed duirng the 1970s and 1980s. Thus, in looking to the future, we must consider the question of whether this is truly a major direction that will shape the nature of research during the coming years or merely a fad growing out of the individualism of the 1970s that will pass in due time. While arguments can be made for both positions, the notion of individuals taking primary responsibility for when, where, why, and how they learn has been one of the most pervasive themes throughout the history of continuing education, both in North America and other parts of the world. Thus, regardless of whether the term *self-directed learning* survives into the next century, it would seem likely that the concept embedded in this term will, in fact, continue to embody the vision of adult learning researchers.

Considerations for Improving Future Research

What are some strategies that might be useful in guiding future efforts to study adult learning? Three possible considerations include using a variety of research designs, increasing emphasis on long-term (or longitudinal) research approaches, and replicating previous studies based on subsequent developments and cross-cultural perspectives.

Research Design. A glance at research during the 1960s and 1970s will reveal that survey studies have been by far the most widely used research approach. Yet, there exists a wide range of designs that can address a variety of questions. For example, survey studies can describe the characteristics of a group. Experimental studies provide an approach for examining the effects of treatments (for example, teaching strategies, elements of classroom environment) on such outcomes as achievement and attitude. Correlational studies examine the ways in which phenomena are related to each other. Qualitative approaches provide a holistic perspective by exploring phenomena from the perspective of those who are being studied. And historical research can help to provide understanding of the context out of which current practices and issues have evolved. Each approach has value for understanding adult learning and can be used without necessarily violating the humanistic focus prevalent throughout much of the continuing education field (Brockett, 1987).

Longitudinal Studies. In building a future research thrust in adult learning, a vision certainly worth considering is the possibility of studying phenomena from a longitudinal perspective. If adult learning is to be understood from a developmental point of view, it will be necessary for researchers to begin focusing on learning-related processes as they evolve over time. For instance, does one's motivation for participation change as one engages in the various developmental transitions of adulthood? This question can only be answered by following a group of adults over time and observing whether or not such changes occur. While expense and long-term commitment are major barriers to longitudinal inquiry, particularly for graduate students and faculty under pressure to publish, careful planning can allow researchers to make an immediate contribution while also providing data on which longitudinal work can be developed.

Replications. As the field of continuing education matures and the research base expands, new ways of thinking about adult learning continue to evolve. Through this maturity, new perspectives and tools emerge that allow us to build on or improve previous approaches to studying research problems. In situations where this occurs, an appropriate strategy may be to replicate earlier research using technical modifications that may present a more accurate representation of the problem area than was possible previously. Similarly, findings from one social setting may not necessarily be relevant to a different milieu; thus, cross-cultural replication can help researchers avoid falling into the trap of overgeneralizing their findings prematurely. While some may see replication research as being inconsistent with a vision of the future, such studies can have a future emphasis, because replication allows for validation and improvement of past work (Darkenwald, 1987b).

Conclusion

As Hiemstra pointed out in Chapter One, a key to the future of continuing education will be the extent to which we take an active role in creating the future. The practical orientation of continuing education has led at times to the relegation of research to a secondary role. However, if the field is to continue to grow and thrive as we move toward the next century, it will be necessary to strive for a better understanding of how adults learn and how to more effectively facilitate the learning process. To achieve this, it will be necessary to be sensitive to both basic research needs and the translation of research findings into practice.

References

Aslanian, C. B., and Brickell, H. M. *Americans in Transition: Life Changes as Reasons for Adult Learning.* New York: College Board, 1980.

Beder, H. W. "Defining the We." *Lifelong Learning: An Omnibus of Practice and Research*, 1985, *8* (5), 2.

Beder, H. W., and Darkenwald, G. G. "Differences Between Teaching Adults and Pre-Adults: Some Propositions and Findings." *Adult Education*, 1982, *32* (3), 142–155.

Brockett, R. G. "Methodological and Substantive Issues in the Measurement of Self-Directed Learning Readiness." *Adult Education Quarterly*, 1985a, *36* (1), 15–24.

Brockett, R. G. "A Response to Brookfield's Critical Paradigm of Self-Directed Adult Learning." *Adult Education Quarterly*, 1985b, *36* (1), 55–59.

Brockett, R. G. "A Perspective on Humanistic Research in Adult Learning." *Lifelong Learning Forum*, 1987, *4* (2), 1, 4–7.

Brookfield, S. D. *Understanding and Facilitating Adult Learning: A Comprehensive Analysis of Principles and Effective Practices.* San Francisco: Jossey-Bass, 1986.

Brunner, E. de S., Wilder, D. S., Kirchner, C., and Newberry, J. C. *An Overview of Adult Education Research.* Washington, D.C.: Adult Education Association of the U.S.A., 1959.

Conti, G. J. "Assessing Teaching Style in Adult Education: How and Why." *Lifelong Learning: An Omnibus of Practice and Research*, 1985a, *8* (8), 7–11, 28.

Conti, G. J. "The Relationship Between Teaching Style and Adult Student Learning." *Adult Education Quarterly*, 1985b, *35* (4), 220–228.

Cross, K. P. *Adults as Learners: Increasing Participation and Facilitating Learning.* San Francisco: Jossey-Bass, 1981.

Daloz, L. A. *Effective Teaching and Mentoring: Realizing the Transformational Power of Adult Learning Experiences.* San Francisco: Jossey-Bass, 1986.

Darkenwald, G. G. "Factor Structure of Differences in Teaching Behavior Related to Adult/Pre-Adult Student Age Status." *Adult Education*, 1982, *32* (4), 197–204.

Darkenwald, G. G. "Assessing the Social Environment of Adult Classes." *Studies in the Education of Adults* (UK), 1987a, *18* (2), 127–136.

Darkenwald, G. G. "Quantitative Methodology: Issues in Comparative Research." Paper presented at the International Conference on Comparative Adult Education, Oxford University, Oxford, England, July 1987b.

Darkenwald, G. G., and Gavin, W. J. "Dropout as a Function of Discrepancies Between Expectations and Actual Experiences of the Classroom Social Environment." *Adult Education Quarterly*, 1987, *37* (3), 152–163.

Darkenwald, G. G., and Hayes, E. "Assessing Adult Attitudes Toward Continuing Education." *International Journal of Lifelong Education*, in press.

Darkenwald, G. G., and Merriam, S. B. *Adult Education: Foundations of Practice.* New York: Harper & Row, 1982.

Darkenwald, G. G., and Valentine, T. "Factor Struture of Deterrents to Participation in Adult Education." *Adult Education Quarterly*, 1985, *35* (4), 177–193.

Darkenwald, G. G., and Valentine, T. "An Empirical Typology of Adults Deterred from Participation in Further Education." *Adult Education Quarterly*, in press.

Dickinson, G., and Rusnell, D. A. "A Content Analysis of *Adult Education*." *Adult Education*, 1971, *21* (3), 177–185.

Elias, J. L., and Merriam, S. *Philosophical Foundations of Adult Education.* Malabar, Fla.: Krieger, 1980.

Essert, P. L. "Adult Education—An Overview." *Review of Educational Research*, 1953, *23* (3), 195–201.

Fisher, J. C. *Educational Attainment, Anomie, Life Satisfaction, and Situational*

Variables as Predictors of Participation in Education Activities by Active Older Adults. Unpublished doctoral dissertation, University of Wisconsin-Milwaukee, 1979.

Garry, M. W. "The Relationship of Anomie, Attitude Toward Adult Education, and Nonparticipation in Formal Adult Education Activities." Paper presented at the annual Adult Education Research Conference, Minneapolis, Minn., 1977.

Gooderham, P. N. "Reference Group Theory and Adult Education." *Adult Education Quarterly*, 1987, *37* (3), 140–151.

Gorham, J. "Differences Between Teaching Adults and Pre-Adults: A Closer Look." *Adult Education Quarterly*, 1985, *35* (4), 194–209.

Guglielmino, L. M. "Development of the Self-Directed Learning Readiness Scale." Unpublished doctoral dissertation, University of Georgia, 1977.

Houle, C. O. "Other Developments." *Review of Educational Research*, 1953, *23* (3), 269–276.

Knowles, M. S. *The Modern Practice of Adult Education.* (Rev. ed.) Chicago: Follett, 1980.

Knox, A. B. *Adult Development and Learning: A Handbook on Individual Growth and Competence in the Adult Years.* San Francisco: Jossey-Bass, 1977.

Knox, A. B. *Helping Adults Learn: A Guide to Planning, Implementing, and Conducting Programs.* San Francisco: Jossey-Bass, 1986.

Long, H. B. "Publication Activity Among Selected Professors of Adult Education." *Adult Education*, 1977, *27* (2), 173–186.

Long, H. B. *Adult Learning: Research and Practice.* New York: Cambridge, 1983.

Moos, R. H. *Evaluating Educational Environments: Procedures, Measures, Findings, and Policy Implications.* San Francisco: Jossey-Bass, 1979.

Murphy, T. W. *Participation of Military Personnel in Public Postsecondary Education Programs: Barriers and Inducements.* Unpublished doctoral dissertation, University of Washington, 1977.

Oddi, L. F. "Development and Validation of an Instrument to Identify Self-Directed Continuing Learners." *Adult Education Quarterly*, 1986, *36* (2), 97–107.

Rubenson, K. *Participation in Recurrent Education.* Paris: Center for Educational Research and Innovation, Organization for Economic Cooperation and Development, 1977.

Scanlan, C. L. *Deterrents to Participation: An Adult Education Dilemma.* Columbus, Ohio: ERIC Clearinghouse on Adult, Career, and Vocational Education, 1986.

Scanlan, C. L., and Darkenwald, G. G. "Identifying Deterrents to Participation in Contininuing Education." *Adult Education Quarterly*, 1984, *34* (3), 155–166.

Shaw, D. M. "Self-Directed Learning and Intellectual Development: A Correlation Study." Unpublished master's thesis, Montana State University, 1987.

Six, J. E., and Hiemstra, R. "The Classroom Learning Scale: A Criterion Measure of the Oddi Continuing Learning Inventory." Paper presented at the Adult Education Research Conference, Laramie, Wyo., May 1987.

Thorndike, E. L. *Adult Learning.* New York: Macmillan, 1928.

Tough, A. *The Adult's Learning Projects: A Fresh Approach to Theory and Practice in Adult Learning.* (2nd ed.) Toronto: Ontario Institute for Studies in Education, 1979.

Zinn, L. "Development of a Valid and Reliable Instrument to Identify a Personal Philosophy of Adult Education." Unpublished doctoral dissertation, Florida State University, 1983.

Ralph G. Brockett is assistant professor of adult education at the Center for Adult Learning Research, Montana State University, Bozeman, Montana. He has worked in continuing education for health and human services professionals, served on the executive committee of the Commission of Professors of Adult Education, and is currently book review editor for Adult Education Quarterly.

Gordon G. Darkenwald is professor of adult and continuing education and codirector of the Center for Adult Development, Rutgers University. He is author or coauthor of several books and monographs, including Last Gamble on Education *(1975) and* Adult Education: Foundations and Practice *(1982). He is former editor of* Adult Education Quarterly *and current editor-in-chief of* New Directions for Continuing Education. *He was a Fulbright senior scholar in Britain in 1986–87.*

Continuing education cannot ignore new instructional technologies without becoming an anachronism. Relevant and accessible programs demand innovative and imaginative delivery systems.

The Role of Technology in Continuing Education

D. Randy Garrison

Discussions of the future, regardless of the focus, are invariably linked to technology, because much of the change we have experienced has been due to various technological innovations. As a result, technology has become a pervasive and persistent topic of discussion that elicits both fascination with, and concern for, its current and future impact on our lives. Since the issues surrounding technology are complex and controversial, every effort has to be made to appreciate the role of technology if we are to influence its impact on our lives. Similarly, it is crucial that any discussion of the future of an enterprise like continuing education must seriously consider the capabilities of various technologies and their role in the adult learning process.

What follows is an assessment of the potential technological benefits to the instructional and learning process in continuing education during the next ten to fifteen years. However, this chapter is not an exotic trip into an imaginary world of future instructional technology, nor is it a utopian or apocalyptic scenario of continuing education in the year 2000. Instead, it is an extrapolation of what we know about the technology we are experimenting with today in order to see where we are heading in the future. Since the decisions we make today will shape the world we will experience in five to twenty years (Cornish, 1977), we need to

R. G. Brockett (ed.). *Continuing Education in the Year 2000.*
New Directions for Continuing Education, no. 36. San Francisco: Jossey-Bass, Winter 1987.

consider current issues and technological capabilities to be able to see what is on the horizon for continuing education.

The chapter will begin with a discussion of two critical issues—access and support—that provide the raison d'etre for adopting new technologies in continuing education. Next, technological developments will be discussed from the perspective of their educational capabilities and possible future role. This will be followed by a discussion of the instructional design process, where technology is an integral component. Finally, the need for an open learning system is described, a system that will provide access and support for learning without the restriction of time and place.

Access and Support

The key to appreciating the role and benefit of technology in continuing education can be found in the issue of access. According to Darkenwald and Merriam (1982), the hallmark of adult education is the intimate relationship between living and learning. However, the fact that participation rates in formal adult education programs across North America range from 15 to 30 pecent (Cross, 1981; Devereaux, 1984) seems to suggest that these programs are not an intimate and integral part of the lives of very many adults. Of course, participation in these formal programs in not indicative of the full extent of adult learning endeavors.

An examination of the literature on self-initiated and planned learning reveals a strong interest in continued learning that appears to be at odds with our participation rates in formal programs. It is reported that anywhere from 75 to over 90 percent of adults engage in at least one purposeful learning project each year (Penland, 1979; Tough, 1979). Further, it is reported that many adults "would welcome more and better help with their self-planned learning" (Tough, 1979, p. 105). Given the apparent desire to learn, and the expressed need for assistance, the question that needs to be asked is, why is there such a discrepancy between desire to learn and actual participation in formal programs? The answer to this seems to be that most of our adult and continuing education programs are, in fact, not accessible in any reasonble manner that would allow adults to experience the previously described intimate relationship between living and learning.

The inaccessibility becomes clearer when one considers that the two most frequently expressed barriers to participation in adult education relate to time and place (Cross, 1981; Waniewicz, 1976). Access to continuing education programs has traditionally meant that learners attend classes at a time and place convenient to the institutions. However, by definition, adults have assumed a number of roles and responsibilities that occupy much of their lives and appear to explain why time and location are real barriers to participating in formal programs. Adults do not always have the luxury of being able to attend, at will, classes scheduled at the convenience of the institution. The challenge, therefore, is to remove and reduce these barriers; and given the finite resources available to continuing education, the best solution appears to be the increased use of technology.

With reference to adult learning, Luskin (1980) has suggested that "if improvements in educational opportunity and access are primary goals of education, wider use of telecommunications technologies are appropriate—and in fact, in the coming decades, necessary" (p. 44). It is also argued that significantly improved access to adult education will necessitate a move away from direct teacher/student interaction. Lowe (1975) has stated that "the need for an extensive application of educational technology is due, even in the richest of countries, to the practical difficulty of meeting even a fraction of the contemporary demand for education by means of a direct teacher/student relationship" (p. 110). In addition, Lowe believes that large-scale continuing education is financially and structurally impossible without the full use of educational technology.

Providing equity of access to continuing education through the use of technology is a critical first step, but it is only part of the picture. Equally important to the continued success of the adult learner is a provision for quality support. Delivery systems must be designed and courseware developed that will allow learning to become an integral part of the learner's activities in the home and workplace. This demands that the psychological and social needs and responsibilities of the adult, which often block learning, be addressed. If technology "is to be an effective educational vehicle for adults, it must integrate with this complex configuration of needs and motivations and not simply facilitate learning at a distance" (Walshok, 1980, p. 97).

To go beyond simply providing access to knowledge, then, is to take a student-centered approach and to personalize learning. Not only must courses and programs be targeted at particular groups, but each individual needs to have considerable control over the how, when, and where of the learning. This increasingly personalized form of learning can only be cost-effective through the intelligent integration of technology, which, in turn, is very much dependent upon continuing educators' appreciating the capabilities of technology and creatively designing delivery systems to meet individual and societal needs. With the communications technology available to us today, the only limitation in designing such systems is our imagination and understanding of the possibilities.

Technological Developments

Before an adequate discussion of the role of technology is possible, we must agree on what the concept of technology means. Unfortunately, technology has too often come to be equated with hardware. However, the generic meaning of the word "does not necessarily imply the use of machines, as many seem to think, but refers to any practical art using scientific knowledge" (Saettler, 1968, p. 6). Therefore, *technology* will be used here to indicate the integration of both hardware and knowledge. In addition, *educational technology* will refer to the scientific application of knowledge and hardware to teaching and learning. Finally, to further clarify our terminology, *media* will be used to refer to only the hardware that is capable of transmitting information.

It is important to emphasize that technology or media may be capable of providing access to educational resources, but technology must never be allowed to take precedence over educational purpose. Too often programs have been developed to make use of some new technology that has had little lasting value. Another common problem with technology is that its merits are often oversold because it was not realized that the success of a course or program is dependent upon the quality of the instructional design. As Heinich, Molenda, and Russell (1982) state, "There is nothing magical about the hardware. The magic, if there is to be magic, stems from the selection of materials according to their usefulness in achieving specific learning objectives and their utilization in ways conducive to applying sound learning principles" (p. 266). However, there is magic in another respect for continuing education, and that is the ability of technology to allow educators to reach out to learners regardless of time and distance.

Distance Education. It is generally agreed that technology has not had a significant influence on how instruction is delivered in the traditional classroom setting (Heinich, 1984). The reason is that technology has been promoted as an adjunct to instruction by service units outside the existing power structures. Teachers "prefer the power relationships the way they are and maintain them by reducing all technologies to the status of 'tools' " (Heinich, 1984, p. 70). This is also true of continuing education, since technology has not generally been used as an integral part of the instructional process with adults.

Boshier (1978) stated some years ago that in the future, "adult education will be characterized by a dizzying array of technologically based and decentralized delivery systems utilizing satellites, intermediate technology, and a broad array of informal opportunities for learning" (p. 1). While efforts have been made to make use of technological resources in continuing education, these efforts have not been pervasive and are not found in the mainstream of the field. The efforts in using this technology have been made by individuals who see themselves largely as distance educators and who are building a field of practice in many ways separate from the larger context of adult education. In distance education the technology is more than an adjunct to the instructional process; it is the main organizational system of linking student and teacher. Distance education provides opportunities for learning to those who do not have the luxury of attending a traditional institutional setting. Distance educators have in recent years been the leaders in technological innovation "and will continue to be a leading edge in the interface between education and technology under the banner of educational opportunity" (Peruniak, 1983, p. 76).

The distinguishing feature of distance education is that it is a means of extending access to education to those who might otherwise be excluded from an educational experience. In this context, three essential criteria are suggested that characterize distance education:

- The majority of educational communication between (among) teacher and student(s) occurs noncontiguously
- Involves two-way communication between (among) teacher and student(s) for the purpose of facilitating and supporting the educational process
- Uses technology to mediate the necessary two-way communication (Garrison and Shale, 1987).

Since teacher and learner are physically separated in distance education, it is clear that communication must be mediated through some form of technology. Distance education is inexorably linked to the technology of delivery. It can be seen as a set of instructional methods based largely on mediated communication capable of extending the influence of the educator beyond the formal institutional setting for the purpose of benefiting the learner through appropriate guidance and support. Without the use of technology, distance education would not exist. This realization underscores the need to understand these technologies.

While an understanding of technology is essential if we are to conceptualize continuing education existing beyond the walls of the formal institutional setting, it cannot adequately be achieved simply through a listing of hardware characteristics. Technology must be seen from an educational perspective, and the essential characteristics capable of providing access and support to learners must be identified. Special attention needs to be directed to the ability of technology to support two-way communication. One of the most promising new technologies for continuing education is the microcomputer.

Microcomputer-Based Learning. If we are to consider the role of technology in continuing education in the year 2000, then special attention must be given to computer-based learning. The current and potential capabilities of computer-assisted learning (CAL) are clearly evident after more than twenty-five years of research. Kearsley, Hunter, and Seidel (1983) have concluded a review of the literature by stating that CAL can be more effective or efficient than traditional instruction and, more important, that we "have just scratched the surface of what can be accomplished with computers in education" (p. 90). For adult and continuing education, "CAL has the capability to cope with the diverse needs and characteristics of the adult learner, to provide alternative means of reaching goals, to provide flexibility for the learner in controlling and pacing the learning experience, to provide for independent and self-directed learning, and to do all of this in a secure, private, and patient manner" (Garrison, 1982, p. 23). Knowles (1983), a proponent of collaborative learning, has even stated that he perceives "the computer to be the most potent tool for adult learning to appear in modern history" (p. 14).

With regard to distance delivery, dramatic new possibilities open up through the use of computer-based learning. Judging from completion rates in distance education, there is good reason to believe that the quality and immediacy of feedback is perhaps the most critical component in the learning process (Garrison, 1987). The computer allows for considerable learner independence and individualization while still providing immediate tutorial interaction and support, although this was considered to be a logical impossibility not long ago (Daniel and Marquis, 1979). The potential of computer-based learning is further enhanced if we consider not only the inevitable reduction in cost and increased power of microcomputers in the future but also the impact of artificial intelligence and quality courseware development. Current examples of intelligent CAL (ICAL) courseware demonstrate its potential to simulate, in a very sophisticated manner, a patient and understanding teacher (Sleeman and Brown, 1982).

ICAL is a result of using artificial intelligence techniques to design a tutorial program that can "choose appropriate examples, provide help where the student needs it, work arbitrary examples chosen by the students, review previous material, provide immediate feedback, provide alternative solutions, and measure the background and progress of the student" (Gable and Page, 1984, p. 267). While ICAL tutorials will become more sophisticated and prevalent in the next decade, the ease of use will be seriously restricted with such existing human-machine interfaces as a keyboard. This barrier will be overcome with innovations in computer voice recognition and speech generation. Although there is great risk in making predictions, it is highly probable that significant breakthroughs will be made by the year 2000, or shortly after, in designing ICAL tutorials that can be interfaced by the learner with natural aural dialogue. As a result of the inevitable advances in ICAL techniques and voice recognition, dialogue between learner and computer tutor will be conducted in a sophisticated and natural manner by the next century.

Emerging communications technology will play an increasingly important role in the delivery of continuing education in the future. However, hardware only provides the potential access to education. The successful application of technology in continuing education is dependent upon integrating technology into an educational system capable of addressing student needs and curriculum requirements. It is clear that we are moving into the microcomputer-based generation of learning, but effective delivery has been shown to be dependent on quality courseware. Similarly, while the laserdisc, integrated with a microprocessor, will likely be the dominant single piece of instructional technology in the 1990s, it will be ineffective and have little influence without the development of quality courseware. The position taken in this chapter is that in most situations it is the technology we know today that will be playing a significant role in continuing education in the year 2000, and the important developments in the next few years will be in software and courseware creation. As Griew (1984) states, "However sophisticated the technology, it is the curriculum that will ultimately make or break any particular activity in the field of continuing education" (p. 370).

Instructional Design Considerations

The systematic and scientific application of media to the learning process is not well developed. What effect media has on learning is poorly understood and no theory exists to guide the selection of media and the design of technological delivery systems that can achieve particular goals. Clark (1983) states categorically that it is the instructional design and the teaching that affect learning and that "media do not influence learning under any conditions" (p. 445). This again emphasizes the point that media or hardware simply carry the message, and it is the design of the interactional support system that is critical in educational technology.

There is, however, another issue to consider when designing technological instruction. The issue is that media by their nature structure and convey messages in different ways. Although Clark (1983) does not state that media per se do not influence learning, he does suggest that instruction may be influenced by media through the adequacy of different media to carry different symbol systems. The central issue is that we must not be preoccupied with technology but, instead, see it as a vehicle of delivery that can structure messages in differing and unique ways. It is the message and the learner that must be of paramount concern in the selection of technological delivery systems. Unfortunately, this creates a dilemma since little theory exists to match media, message, and learner. As Heinich, Molenda, and Russell (1982) state, "The great quest in the field of media and technologies of instruction is to find ways of matching individual learners with the appropriate subject matter, pitched at the right level, and presented in a compatible medium at the optimal pace in the most meaningful sequence" (p. 311). This is, of course, no easy task.

While these comments may sound discouraging regarding the design of technologically based instructional systems, there is a short-term solution to this dilemma. The solution is based upon the belief that continuing education should be learner-centered and the learner should have considerable control over the process. There are no substitutes for instructional design; certain methods work for particular learners under specific conditions (Heinich, Molenda, and Russell, 1982). As a result, there has been a shift in focus toward individualized and personalized instruction, with individuals determining or developing to varying degrees their own learning objectives and activities.

Learning Styles

The limited generalizability of particular instructional methods is also evident in the research into learning styles. Few definitive conclusions have been reached regarding congruency among preferred learning styles and instructional methods. Pratt (1983), states that "we are lacking research that extends the implications of learning styles to instruction. We have available an array of instruments, each assessing some aspect of learning style, but little advice or evidence on how to apply the results within adult learning environments" (p. 63).

Learning style concerns an individual's preferred way of learning. Although there is general agreement that experience and maturity foster a wider range of individual differences, adult learners have the ability to adapt to a variety of learning methods (Conti and Welborn, 1986). As Dixon (1985) suggests, preferred learning styles do "not imply that these are the only or perhaps the best ways for the individual to learn a given subject matter" (p. 16). The best strategy seems to be to help learners understand their styles, to use a variety of instructional methods, and to encourage learners to stretch by using styles other than those preferred (Dixon, 1985). It is suggested here that the only realistic way of providing such choice is through the use of technology.

Clearly, technology can provide access to learning where it previously did not exist, but it also has the potential to improve the quality of learning support by individualizing learning and recognizing preferred learning styles. By providing a variety of learning methods, a better balance of teacher and learner influence over the learning process can be achieved. Given our limited understanding of matching media, methods, and such individual learner characteristics as learning style, perhaps the most expedient approach is to provide more individualized learning methods based on new technologies and shift more of the responsibility for learning to the individual. This is not to exclude, however, group methods of learning, either at a distance or face-to-face. Curriculum and learner needs will demand a full range of delivery and learning methods that are designed to provide access and support.

Although providing greater diversity and choice of learning approaches through technology is a sound strategy, better methods should also be found to study how adults learn. This issue is addressed more fully by Brockett and Darkenwald in Chapter Three. Technology has the capability to go beyond providing access and support for learning by playing an indispensable role in studying how adults learn. It has been noted how little we know about applying learning style theory and how to best use media and technology in delivering instruction. However, through the provision of learning choices using technology, an opportunity is created to efficiently and unobtrusively gather data about the learning process. These data can be used to generate theory that will eventually guide and direct the design and delivery of adult and continuing education. Such an approach, by its very nature, will also have the added benefit of integrating research and practice to a greater degree and may help reduce the gap between research and practice.

An Open Learning System

In an analysis of adult learning in a rapidly changing society, Thompkins (1982) argues for an extension of continuing education opportunities through increased flexibility and decreased emphasis on courses and classes. Such a future vision will be largely dependent on the intelligent integration of new learning technologies with traditional methodologies. Access to learning through open learning concepts and structures made possible by technological innovations represents increased educational opportunities for potential continuing education participants. To realize such a future, however, emphasis must be given to the development of organizational structures that can incorporate new educational technologies.

Continuing education must become more open and outward-looking to continue to meet the changing needs of adult learners. If continuing education is to continue to reach out to new audiences, innovative, technologically based delivery systems must be developed. Future delivery structures must reflect the concept of an open learning system. Open learning is a flexible system where individuals may learn how, when, and where it suits them. An open learning system is concerned with both access to education and support of the learning process. Such a system is very much learner-centered and makes use of both traditional classrooms and societal settings, as well as using a variety of methods that may or may not be technologically based. Although technology is an integral part of an open learning system, a variety of methods are used that are appropriate for the content, situation, and individual. As a result, there will be a blurring of the boundaries between traditional and independent study that can only be of benefit to all continuing learners.

Lifelong Learning

While there is much debate as to what is meant by lifelong learning, the real task is attempting to implement such a far-reaching concept.

In attempting to operationalize the concept of lifelong learning, Mocker and Spear (1982) identify control of the learning process as the primary characteristic for understanding and implementing this concept. Their model suggests that lifelong learning includes formal, informal, nonformal, and self-directed learning that ranges from strong institutional control to full learner control. But it can be argued that we are not doing enough to provide and support learning controlled largely by the learner in a variety of settings.

Economic forces are constraining the expansion of our traditional delivery systems at a time when the demands for continuing education and training are increasing. It is clear that if lifelong learning is to become a reality, then a way must be found to meet the learning needs of an increasingly greater proportion of our society. Miller (1982), in a discussion of communication technology for continuing educators, cites Joseph (1979) in suggesting "that traditional education will continue to experience extreme stress because it is labor intensive and because of the rapid growth of knowledge. There is mounting pressure to increase productivity in education. This pressure will result in distributing the delivery of education along a lifelong learning continuum and in moving toward the electronic delivery of education" (p. 1). Not only must learning be a lifetime pursuit, but it must be supported beyond the walls of formal institutions for two reasons: First, it satisfies a necessary requirement of being cost-effective, and second, it better meets the learning needs of adults by reaching out to them in their home and workplace.

We will have open learning systems when every means possible is used to provide access and support in the learning process for all segments of society, when personal interests and fears are put aside to critically and synoptically analyze what technology can do for the adult learner, when we begin to restructure and decentralize the delivery of continuing education, and when we all begin to take a rational and accountable approach to creating a better future. And it is these open learning concepts and systems that will allow learning to become a natural part of living and ultimately show the way to facilitating lifelong learning for all.

Conclusion

It has been argued that a basic reason for considering the increased use of technology in continuing education is the obligation and need to reach a greater proportion of adult learners. It is not enough to use technology to support learning in a more efficient and interesting manner for the small and generally privileged group of adult learners who are able to attend traditional classroom programs. Distance educators have taken the leadership in the use of technology to reach out to adult learners without regard to geographic location. With regard to distance education, Moore (1986) states that the "leaders in our field were men and women with a vision that modern technology could be used to free people from constraints on their learning—the constraints of geographic isolation, being housebound, being disabled, or having to hold down a job and therefore not being able to study. Their ends were human, though the means they employed were technological" (p. 22). The technology used to deliver education at a distance will be the technology having the greatest impact on continuing education in the future. However, to go beyond simple access to learning, the role of technology in instructional design must be clearly understood. That is, support of learning through quality courseware and curriculum design is essential, and it is in this area that the real challenge is to be found when integrating technology into open learning systems.

The role of technology in continuing education by the year 2000 will have influenced all aspects of this enterprise. Greater use of technology by continuing educators to provide equity of access and ongoing support and interaction during the learning process will be demanded by students and necessitated by economic constraints and competition from private educational entrepreneurs. Continuing education will see the greatest growth and change of any educational sector in the 1990s. The challenge for continuing educators is to integrate the new technologies into a coherent and functional delivery system that is open to all adult learners.

In the future, it will be the variety of provision and the quality of interaction with the teacher and learning materials that will attract and sustain the continuing education learner. To have a viable role in the continuing education enterprise, delivery systems will be required to integrate learning into the life of the adult with a minimum of disruption and inconvenience. The key to integrating learning with the various roles and responsibilities of adult life is communication systems. If continuing education does not adopt communications technology, entrepreneurs will develop and market their own materials. On the other hand, today's continuing education institutions can move from the periphery of the educational scene and become a major player in the economic and cultural development of our society if continuing educators strive to imagine and create educational delivery systems based on the potential of technology to bring individuals together electronically.

References

Boshier, R. W. "The Future of Adult and Continuing Education: Purposes and Issues." Paper presented at the Annual Conference of the Canadian Association for University Continuing Education, Moncton, New Brunswick, June 14, 1978.

Clark, R. E. "Reconsidering Research on Learning from Media." *Review of Educational Research,* 1983, *53* (4), 445-459.

Conti, G. J., and Welborn, R. B. "Teaching-Learning Styles and the Adult Learner." *Lifelong Learning: An Omnibus of Practice and Research,* 1986, *9* (8), 20-24.

Cornish, E. *The Study of the Future.* Washington, D.C.: World Future Society, 1977.

Cross, K. P. *Adults as Learners: Increasing Participation and Facilitating Learning.* San Francisco: Jossey-Bass, 1981.

Daniel, J. S., and Marquis, C. "Interaction and Independence: Getting the Mixture Right." *Teaching at a Distance,* 1979, *14,* 29-43.

Darkenwald, G. G., and Merriam, S. B. *Adult Education: Foundations of Practice.* New York: Harper & Row, 1982.

Devereaux, M. S. *One in Every Five: A Survey of Adult Education in Canada.* Ottawa, Ontario: Statistics Canada, 1984.

Dixon, N. M. "The Implementation of Learning Style Information." *Lifelong Learning: An Omnibus of Practice and Research,* 1985, *9* (3), 16-18, 26.

Gable, A., and Page, C. V. "The Use of Artificial Intelligence Techniques in Computer-Assisted Instruction: An Overview." In D. F. Walker and R. D. Hess (eds.), *Instructional Software: Principles and Perspectives for Design and Use.* Belmont, Calif.: Wadsworth, 1984.

Garrison, D. R. "Microcomputers and CAL in Adult Education." *Lifelong Learning: The Adult Years,* 1982, *5* (10), 22-23.

Garrison, D. R. "Researching Dropout in Distance Education: Some Directional and Methodological Considerations." *Distance Education,* 1987, *8* (1), 95-101.

Garrison, D. R., and Shale, D. "Mapping the Boundaries of Distance Education: Problems in Defining the Field." *American Journal of Distance Education,* 1987, *1* (1), 7-13.

Griew, S. "Prospects for the Future." In T. Craig and E. A. Archer (eds.), *Technological Innovation: University Roles.* London: The Association of Commonwealth Universities, 1984.

Heinich, R. "The Proper Study of Instructional Technology." *Educational Communication and Technology,* 1984, *32* (2), 67-87.

Heinich, R., Molenda, M., and Russell, J. D. *Instructional Media and the New Technologies of Instruction.* New York: Wiley, 1982.

Joseph, E. C. "Long-Term Electronic Technology Trends: Forecast on Education." Paper presented to the Congress of the United States, House of Representatives, Committee on Education and Labor, Subcommittee on Education and Labor and Subcommittee on Elementary, Secondary, and Vocational Education, 1979. (ED 179 878)

Kearsley, G., Hunter, B., and Seidel, R. J. "Two Decades of Computer Based Instruction Projects: What Have We Learned?" *T.H.E. Journal,* 1983, *10* (3), 90-94.

Knowles, M. "Memorandum." *Training and Development Journal,* 1983, *5,* 14.

Lowe, J. *The Education of Adults: A World Perspective.* Paris: UNESCO Press, 1975.

Luskin, B. "Telecommunications: A Prism of Access for Adult Learning." *T.H.E. Journal,* 1980, *7* (5), 43-50.

Miller, J. "Questions About Communications Technologies for Educators: An Introduction." In N. Singer (ed.), *Communications Technologies: Their Effect on Adult, Career, and Vocational Education.* Columbus, Ohio: ERIC Clearinghouse on Adult, Career, and Vocational Education, 1982.

Mocker, D. W., and Spear, G. E. *Lifelong Learning: Formal, Nonformal, Informal, and Self-Directed.* Columbus, Ohio: ERIC Clearinghouse on Adult, Career, and Vocational Education, 1982. (ED 220 723)

Moore, M. "Self-Directed Learning and Distance Education." *Journal of Distance Education,* 1986, *1,* 7–24.

Penland, P. "Self-Initiated Learning." *Adult Education,* 1979, *29* (3), 170–179.

Peruniak, G. S. "Interactive Perspective in Distance Education." *Distance Education,* 1983, *4* (1), 63–79.

Pratt, D. "Learning Style and Andragogical Instruction: A Pilot Study." Paper presented at the Canadian Association for Studies in Adult Education Conference, Toronto, June 21, 1983.

Saettler, P. *A History of Instructional Technology.* New York: McGraw-Hill, 1968.

Sleeman, D., and Brown, J. S. (eds.). *Intelligent Tutoring Systems.* New York: Academic Press, 1982.

Thompkins, E. "Adult Education in a Changing Society." In N. Costello and M. Richardson (eds.), *Continuing Education for the Post-Industrial Society.* Milton Keynes, England: Open University Press, 1982.

Tough, A. *The Adult's Learning Projects: A Fresh Approach to Theory and Practice in Adult Learning.* (2nd ed.) Austin, Tex.: Learning Concepts, 1979.

Walshok, M. L. "Summary: Some Unanswered Questions About Telecommunications and Adult Learning." In M. N. Chamberlain (ed.), *Providing Continuing Education by Media and Technology.* New Directions for Continuing Education, no. 5. San Francisco: Jossey-Bass, 1980.

Waniewicz, I. *Demand for Part-Time Learning in Ontario.* Toronto: Ontario Institute for Studies in Education, 1976.

D. Randy Garrison is associate professor and director of distance education at the University of Calgary. His primary area of research in adult education is participation. He also writes on theoretical aspects of distance education and is currently implementing and evaluating a multifunction microcomputer enhancement of audio teleconferencing for adult postsecondary education in Alberta.

Management may be the single most important factor in the success of continuing education now and in the coming century.

Changing Practices in Continuing Education Management

Douglas H. Smith

Rarely, if ever, has a new basic institution, a new leading group, a new central function, emerged as fast as has management since the turn of the century. Rarely in human history has a new institution proven indispensable so quickly [Drucker, 1974, p. 12].

Change in higher education has had a substantial impact upon the academic support and service sectors, such as admissions, development, student affairs, and continuing education. Higher costs, less income, more competition for students, lower enrollments of traditional college-age students, and increased enrollments of women, minorities, and older adults have placed these units on alert at virtually every college and university. Traditionally considered necessary but secondary functions of the institution, they are now in the middle of a variety of strategies and plans to increase revenues, maintain costs, and attract more students.

Continuing education programs have been particularly singled out as a rich source of both new revenue and new students. They are being asked to assume a more active role in programming and marketing, but

R. G. Brockett (ed.). *Continuing Education in the Year 2000.*
New Directions for Continuing Education, no. 36. San Francisco: Jossey-Bass, Winter 1987.

usually without additional resources or substantial change in present policies or practices regarding availability of faculty, equipment, or space. And yet there are numerous examples of thriving, highly successful continuing education programs throughout the nation. With few exceptions the available resources and operational policies differ little from less successful programs. The successful programs operate under similar constraints but look primarily at their potential.

For this chapter, numerous interviews were conducted with deans and directors of successful, productive continuing education programs from public and private colleges and universities. Everyone was carefully questioned regarding the reasons for their successful operation. None indicated special privileges or support. No one identified a president or provost who gave exceptional assistance. Indeed, many stated they have to periodically educate these executives on the real potential and limitations of the continuing education program.

In sum, there is a primary, and often the only, reason for these programs being successful: effective management. While laws, regulations, personalities, and trends have an impact upon an individual enterprise, the creation, improvement, or destruction of the enterprise is determined by how resources are managed.

Numerous definitions exist for *management*, but the one most apropos for our discussion is "making resources productive." Continuing education programs may have similar amounts of funds and other resources, but the successful programs have maximized the productivity of their given resources far in excess of the norm.

Why? What ingredients have been brought together that result in successful, productive continuing education programming? The interviews with successful continuing education managers identified three basic strengths: they achieve success through innovation and creativity, shifting resources from old or declining programs to new and more productive ones, and continuously improving the productivity of their resources.

This chapter examines management within the framework of how it is carried out by successful continuing education managers. A number of issues are discussed that collectively have a substantial positive impact upon programming. The chapter concludes with a discussion of selected issues continuing education managers need to address today, since in order to assure the survival of continuing education during the present and coming turbulent times, continuing education programs will need to be more successfully managed now.

Three Major Functions of Continuing Education Management

Management texts traditionally break out managerial activities into the five functions of planning, organizing, staffing, directing, and controlling. While applicable to continuing education, these functions need to be viewed as processes and grouped under more relevant terms. Within the framework of management as defined above (making resources productive), three major functions of management that need to be implemented for growth into the twenty-first century are managing key resources, entrepreneurship (or intrapreneurship), and administration. Each of these is examined from the perspective of its application to continuing education management.

Managing Resources. Drucker (1980), in a discussion of contemporary management, identified three critical resources that, in the present transition to a more service-oriented, information-based society, will need to be consistently managed for effective productivity. They include the management of human resources (people), capital, and physical assets. Each has to be managed separately and differently.

People. "Managers need to realize that they are being paid for enabling people to do the work for which those people are being paid" (Drucker, 1980, p. 24). The importance of this axiom is critical in those enterprises, like continuing education, whose productivity is extremely dependent upon the individual productivity of people. It is the manager's job to ask everyone in the organization, including themselves: "What do we do in this organization, and what do I do that helps you in doing what you are paid for? And, conversely, what do I do that hampers you?"

Asking these crucial questions emphasizes the fact that people are hired because they can do a specific job better than anyone else. Managers cannot make the erroneous assumption that they know how each job should be performed. For most work the only true expert is the person who does the job. Thus, the productivity of human resources, of people, requires that they be assigned where the maximum potential for results can be realized. This is discussed more fully in the section on leadership.

Capital. Simply stated, the management of capital is the management of money—how it is accumulated and how it is spent. Managers of public and nonprofit enterprises too often give only cursory attention to program finances, to the management of their capital. Managers must know where the money is being invested. They must know where the money really is before they can start managing what it buys and produces.

It seems, initially, like a simple task. An annual budget is prepared, and when approved, accounts are opened with a balance from which payments are drawn. The decisions and strategies behind the budget, however, are crucial, with important decisions being made on where the money will come from, and what activities and programs will be endorsed through the commitment of funds.

Physical Assets. Like capital, the management of the physical assets of the continuing education program is too often given cursory attention and almost totally unaccounted for in most continuing education programs. Continuing education managers must think through what the key physical assets are and require productivity goals to be met in order to ensure the efficient operation of these assets, just like any other resource. The buildings, classrooms, offices—the campus—are primary physical assets that establish the image and identity of the educational enterprise.

Entrepreneurship. The second primary function in the management of continuing education is one that usually is identified under the rubric of program development, marketing, or promotion. A more inclusive, more descriptive term is *entrepreneurship*—taking direct responsibility for creative innovation. This function goes far beyond program development and marketing. It is the taking of ideas and creating the dream; making the idea become reality. It is the taking of risks, albeit calculated risks.

Clearly, the successful continuing education leaders interviewed for this chapter were innovators and entrepreneurs. Just as often as ideas for programs evolved out of working with individuals or groups that came forward with an idea, these leaders initiated ideas and sought out appropriate groups to test the idea and gather interest and support. Equally important was the encouragement of their staff to be entrepreneurially directed. They supported risk taking through sharing responsibility and involvement.

What are the characteristics of entrepreneurial managers? Pinchot (1985) coined the term *intrapreneur,* referring to the "dreamers who do" within an organization. He identified a number of key factors that describe these doers. Entrepreneurs/intrapreneurs in an organization:

- Are goal-oriented and self-motivated, but also respond to organizational recognition; they want freedom and access to available resources
- Usually know the business intimately; they may have more business acumen than managerial or political skill
- Are self-confident, optimistic, and courageous; they may be critical of the system but believe they can outwit it
- Are sensitive to important others, both inside and outside the organization; they sell insiders on the need to try an idea but also focus on the target population (the client or customer)
- Often do their own market research; they use intuitive market evaluation, such as talking with potential target population(s), and form opinions that are often quite accurate
- Are adept at getting others to agree to their dream or private vision; they are fairly patient and willing to compromise, but they still are doers
- Like moderate risk, and may not be afraid of being fired; thus, they see little personal risk.

The continuing education leaders interviewed exhibited a majority of these characteristics. They liked being entrepreneurial. They enjoyed, some would say thrived on, taking an idea and running with it. If the idea was successful, they were pleased, of course, but they were often already working on another idea and were committed to the new project. If the idea was not successful, it was often realized early enough to not be a great loss. The key activity was innovation, the shift of resources from old and declining activities and programs to new and more productive ones.

A word should be said about sticking one's neck out. The successful continuing education managers had been in their positions an average of five years. They knew the institution and politics well enough to know what innovations they could try, because they had taken the time to understand the organizational culture of their institution. Once they believed they understood it, they usually tried carefully selected, innovative programs with little or no fanfare until they were convinced the programs were successful, as defined by what the institution deemed successful.

Administration. If key resources are to be effectively managed, and if entrepreneurial ventures are to be validated as successful, there needs to be a system of measures and records—an administrative system—to support successes and quickly identify losses. *Administration* has been used interchangeably with *management* to describe the traditional functions of planning, organizing, staffing, leading, and controlling (for example, Eble, 1978; Strother and Klus, 1982). As used in this chapter, *administration* refers to two key functions: planning—the development of general goals and achievable objectives; and control—the task of assuring the activities conducted are providing the desired results. Thus, administration is more narrowly defined than management, as it refers to the specific functions of collecting, storing, and transmitting needed information to determine as clearly as possible whether program objectives are met and goals achieved.

The administrative function consists of two sequential activities that are basically the same regardless of the program. These activities, the establishment of standards and the measurement of performance, are addressed below. Both must be developed and implemented in order to monitor the resources and maintain a balance between being too conservative and taking too many risks.

Establish Standards or Targets. Any target or standard is better than nothing, even if it is ultimately realized the target was too low or too high. Standards and targets can be grouped into three forms of measures: quantitative—expected enrollments, expected registrations or inquiries from advertisements and marketing campaigns, numbers of programs conducted by the staff; monetary—expected revenues, projected expenses, cancellation if losses reach a specified point; and qualitative—end-of-program evaluation, perceived satisfaction, assessment of knowledge or skills gained, and, when appropriate, evaluation of performance by participants' supervisors.

Two guidelines should be followed when establishing standards or targets. First, develop flexible targets, by estimating as accurately as possible the expected level of such items as income, enrollments, and programs, and then establishing a range between a minimally acceptable level and maximum possible level. Second, keep standards and targets confidential, using them as internal, personal measures of productivity. When the targets are achieved or exceeded, the large enrollments, the number of successful programs, or the favorable reaction to a quality program will be known and acknowledged. If they are not achieved, only a few of the staff will know, and revisions and adjustments for better estimates can be made.

Measure Actual Performance Against the Standards. Measures can range from personal observation, or "management by walking around" (Peters and Austin, 1985); to performance evaluation, or management by objectives; to reacting to data exceeding projected ranges, or management by exception. It requires the establishment of an information or feedback system to know the impact of the actions taken. Like the standard or targets, feedback can also be grouped into quantitative data (actual enrollments, registrations received, programs completed), monetary data (gross revenue, net revenue, actual expenses), and qualitative data (knowledge gained, assessments by the learners and supervisors, spin-offs of additional requests for programs and services).

From quantitative and monetary data, ratios can be used to analyze program productivity. Examples of such ratio analyses are expenses per revenue received (E/R), expenses per instructional hours (E/IH) or continuing education units (E/CEU), registrations per cost of advertising (R/A), and enrollments per programming hours by coordinating staff (E/PH). Ratio analysis has been questioned by some regarding its accuracy and criticized for requiring a considerable amount of data, but others advocate that such measures be tried. No longer can the continuing education leader afford to manage by whim. The future of the field is being questioned, and continuing education leaders cannot afford to be viewed as mediocre managers.

Changing Practices in Continuing Education Management

Having described the three basic processes of contemporary continuing education management, some key issues need to be addressed within the framework of changing management practice. These include the role of profit, the real costs of programming, developing strategies, not just plans, and sharing leadership.

The Central Role of Profit. Long an issue in the field, the question of whether or not continuing education should be expected to make a profit needs to be addressed. I advocate that continuing education be a revenue-producing business, an entrepreneurial, profit-centered enterprise within a nonprofit organization. Nearly every one of the continuing education leaders interviewed indicated the need to generate a specified profit, a budgeted amount of revenue beyond expenses. There are four primary reasons for this. The profit claimed to be made may not be an actuality if all the expenses, such as charge-backs, are assigned to continuing education. If they are, most so-called profits would quickly disappear.

A second reason for making a specified profit is the continued likelihood that funding for higher education in general, and continuing education in particular, will not be increasing. Earmarked funds for special projects, such as employability training, high-tech training, and health-related continuing education, will continue, but the days of unquestioned support for salaries and support services, for continuing education funds from federal higher education acts, and for general support from foundations are essentially over. Further, the competition for any existing funds will be very intense, not only from organizations outside the university but also from units within the university.

The third reason has not been as crucial in recent years. Although it is generally ignored in most nonprofit units, it still warrants consideration. Profit made from revenue where the market is inflated, or where the resources were purchased at pre-inflationary prices, is really windfall profit that should be enjoyed but not counted on. Most continuing education programs have experienced the course or program that took off unexpectedly and large revenues were realized. They have also often realized lower profits when the program is too frequently repeated.

A recent example is the tremendous response for microcomputer courses. Many who got in early reaped large profits, thanks often to the approval to purchase the necesary equipment and also to the purchase of the right equipment (some programs folded simply for buying microcomputers that the consumer did not buy). Now, many continuing education programs are getting out of microcomputer courses because of the cost to update the equipment and the tremendous competition from outside entrepreneurs and computer stores. In other words, while windfall profits are always possible, because of competition from other providers for capturing the hot markets, the opportunity for making such profits is vanishing.

A final major reason for the need to design profit-making continuing education programs is perhaps the most important because it acknowledges that no organization ever makes a profit. Good management includes earning today the costs of staying in business tomorrow. As stated by Drucker (1980, p. 29), profit "is an accounting illusion. . . .

There are no profits; there are only the deferred costs of staying in business.''

Profit should be considered a capital resource to be allocated for future growth and development. It should not be automatically considered funds to be returned to the general fund of the university or college. Profit is the cost of staying in business. It is the seed corn for tomorrow, the investment funds for the healthy continuing education program in the twenty-first century.

The Real Costs of Continuing Education Programming. Earlier in this chapter the importance of knowing the cost of a program's physical assets was discussed. Unlike in business, where units are considered a profit center and are accountable for all expenses, most colleges and universities do not charge internal units for many costs. The practice of not making charges, or charge-backs, for these nonprogram expenses or resources is accepted by colleges and universities because of the present practice of centralized control of these resources and the complexity involved in developing equitable formulas for charge-backs. However, the days of free services and resources are numbered. Costs for office space, heat, light, computer time, and a percentage of other office and staff expenses that are needed in order to make the continuing education program run within the college and university will increasingly be budgeted, or charged back, for remuneration.

During the double-digit inflation days of the late 1970s, a university in the midwestern United States developed a charge-back formula. When the continuing education unit was given its percentage of costs for capital resources and support services and these expenses were added to the existing expenditures the unit was responsible for, it was quickly realized that the present level of program revenue paid for less than half of the total cost of the continuing education program.

The response was obvious. The formulas were reviewed, strongly questioned, and the contribution of continuing education to the overall good of the university (such as credit enrollments, good public relations, service to the community) was strongly stated. The rationale was supported and the charge-backs were not made. The experience, however, unnerved the continuing education staff, and greater attention has been given since then to both knowing the real costs of running the program and generating revenue that is closer to real costs. In the coming years, this will be a practice many other continuing education programs will have to deal with. With the increasing sophistication of accounting procedures, all units within the organization, particularly revenue-generating units like continuing education, will be charged for all services and resources used.

Developing Strategies for Ventures Rather than Plans for Growth. Over the last twenty years, the concept of planning has proven to be highly effective. Additionally, good planning has resulted in growth.

Planning and growth, however, have been largely based on the continuation of trends and practices within fairly narrow, predictable ranges, with few sudden shifts and changes. Continuing education has largely been the only program of its kind in the community and, up until the late 1970s, has essentially been left alone and allowed to do whatever the unit wanted as long as it has been successful. Programs have grown, to a large degree, in a vacuum. There has been little competition.

All has changed, and what can be counted on is one unique event after another. In colleges and universities, the pressure of declining enrollments has introduced a survival mentality, with institutions that previously never gave a thought to continuing education now making it a major activity. Presidents, vice presidents, and other central administrators are giving mixed signals because they really do not know what to do. Within the communities outside the institution, adult learning is now big business, with many organizations developing extensive human resource development programs and hiring consultants, including college and university faculty. They no longer rely on the continuing education unit because of the (unfortunately, too often correct) perception that they can be more focused if they do it themselves. The increased use of computers in instruction has established a major base in business and industry, as opposed to higher education, because of the high cost of the equipment and resistance by faculty. One unique event after another.

Unique events cannot be planned, but strategies can be developed that anticipate the areas in which changes are likely to occur. Planning tries to optimize the trends of today. Strategies take advantage of the unforeseen and unforeseeable.

Strategies require venture and risks. Ventures must be tried but strategically developed. The previous example of the ventures made in microcomputer education frequently proved very successful. Examples of possible ventures include contract programming with area businesses and associations, intensive certificate programs in state-of-the-art topics, computer-based training, establishing cable classrooms, using electronic bulletin boards for learning purposes, becoming a part of global learning groups, investing in satellite downlink capabilities, and conducting seminars on futuristics. What is important is to do less planning and more venturing, to take some risks, to think strategically.

It may also mean thinking small. With the continuing trend away from general education to highly defined instruction for specified populations, continuing education needs to carefully define its strengths and who has need of them. The middle-of-the-road, general continuing education program may commit important resources to nonstrategic activities, resulting in mediocrity. By remaining functionally small, the continuing education unit may serve well the people who want an education that can only be provided by a few.

To think strategically is to clearly identify what can be done well and, equally important, what "value" means to the people to be served. Strategic thinking looks outward, focusing on keeping a program in step with the changing environment. It requires, as emphasized by Keller (1984, p. 145), the need to keep "two incongruous bodies of facts and ideas—internal aspirations and external conditions—in mind at the same time and act to move the institution ahead nevertheless."

Learning to Share Leadership. As stated previously, management is defined as making resources productive. Increasingly, it is becoming recognized that the most critical resources in any organization are the people, the human resources. The leadership of people has become critically important. Over the past five years a number of best-selling books have shown that the key ingredient to successful organizations is recognition and support of the client or customer and the people within the organization serving them (for example, Peters and Waterman, 1982; Peters and Austin, 1985; Blanchard and Johnson, 1984). The primary message of these authors is that the best investment for managers is the time they spend with the people they manage.

This is important for every organization but critical in people-intensive professional organizations like higher education, the prototype of knowledge organizations. While capital equipment and physical resources have substantially increased in colleges and universities, the most important resource remains the people serving the learners—the faculty, directors, coordinators, and support staff.

Continuing education managers must enable highly educated people to be productive—people who have chosen, at this point in their careers, to work in continuing education to actualize their personal goals. Managing such a staff is like leading a double-headed monster, seeking organizational productivity from people who are dedicated to their discipline or profession rather than the organization. While acknowledging this, it still remains the responsibility of the manager to make sure these professionals are held accountable, develop standards, set goals and objectives, and judge their performance against these accepted standards and objectives.

How best can a manager lead professionals? Collectively the leading texts in leadership suggest that managers should know the strengths of the people they manage in order to facilitate and enable those strengths. It requires the development of an environment where people are challenged to think through what they can do to improve what they are already doing. It requires adoption of the Zen concept of learning: one learns in order to do better what one already knows how to do well. People should be encouraged to be their own leaders. Thus, managers must learn to relinquish sole leadership. They must learn to relinquish some leadership responsibilities to those they lead.

This may prove to be difficult in the coming years. While managers are responsible for the productivity of assigned resources and programs, the work will be performed by highly educated professionals and, increasingly, by people and units who are not fully responsible to the manager. The continuing education leaders interviewed repeatedly emphasized the increasing role of managing programs whose operations are carried out by units being managed by other persons. As one respondent indicated, no longer can continuing education be a piece of the pie, part of but separate from other units. It must be an ingredient in the recipe that makes up the pie. It must be a facilitator of the entrepreneurial efforts of the entire institution. Such a role is highly influential and has a great impact if done right, but it requires a leader that enables leadership and does not want to be the leader.

Such a leader is not powerful but leads with strength. A strong leader encourages the strengths of others. As stated by Carse (1986, p. 31), "Power refers to the freedom persons have within limits, strength to the freedom persons have with limits." An appropriate analogy for such leadership is the small instrumental ensemble. Each player is equal, even though there is always a leader.

Managing for the Twenty-First Century

The central role of management is to make the resources as productive as possible, particularly in this time of turbulence. The probability of any substantive change in trends and directions is not likely. What is likely is the exacerbation of the present trend toward a highly competitive environment for continuing education. Thus, the key variable, the one ingredient that will result in those programs being successful and thriving in the opening years of the twenty-first century is effective management of present programs. The task will be challenging, often with little reward and recognition from others. This was understood centuries ago by Machiavelli when he stated, "There is nothing more difficult to carry out, nor more doubtful of success, nor more dangerous to handle, than to initiate a new order of things. For the reformer has enemies in all those who profit by the old order, and only lukewarm defenders in all those who would profit by the new order, these lukewarmers arising partly from fear of their adversaries, who have the laws in their favor, and partly from the incredulity of mankind, who do not truly believe in anything new until they have actual experience of it."

The challenge is to be a reformer, to initiate a new order. Competent continuing education managers will take the responsibility for the productivity of available resources. They will be entrepreneurs, developing profit-centered enterprises in a nonprofit organization where entrepreneurial endeavors are likely to be questioned. They will develop

66

functional administrative systems that assure quality control. They will recognize and support the strengths of the people they manage, sharing leadership in order to be a leader. Then, these managers will be managing a program and staff that eagerly looks forward to, rather than walking backward into, the twenty-first century.

References

Blanchard, K., and Johnson, S. *The One Minute Manager.* New York: Berkley Books, 1984.

Carse, J. P. *Finite and Infinite Games.* New York: Free Press, 1986.

Drucker, P. F. *Management: Tasks and Responsibilities.* New York: Harper & Row, 1974.

Drucker, P. F. *Managing in Turbulent Times.* New York: Harper & Row, 1980.

Eble, K. E. *The Art of Administration: A Guide for Academic Administrators.* San Francisco: Jossey-Bass, 1978.

Keller, G. *Academic Strategy.* Baltimore, Md.: Johns Hopkins University Press, 1984.

Peters, T. J., and Austin, N. *A Passion for Excellence.* New York: Random House, 1985.

Peters, T. J., and Waterman, R. G., Jr. *In Search of Excellence.* New York: Warner Books, 1982.

Pinchot, G. *Intrapreneuring: How to Become an Entrepreneur Without Having to Leave the Organization.* New York: Harper & Row, 1985.

Strother, G. B., and Klus, J. P. *Administration of Continuing Education.* Belmont, Calif.: Wadsworth, 1982.

Douglas H. Smith is associate professor of adult education and human resource development at Florida International University in Miami, Florida. He has also served as dean of continuing education at Florida International, and associate dean of the College for Continuing Education at Drake University.

Issues related to professionalization of the field will be crucial in the year 2000.

Professionalization as an Issue for Continuing Education

Ronald M. Cervero

A Possible Future

It is the year 2020. The federal government has finally passed the Adult Educare Bill, as the result of an intense lobbying effort by a political action committee of continuing educators. Now, any adult who wants to develop literacy skills or obtain a high school diploma can do so by enrolling in a national system of adult literacy classes. Of course, there is a $200 fee to be paid by students every semester in which they enroll to defray some of the cost of this multibillion-dollar program.

Members of Congress from economically deprived districts decry this fee because it has created two classes of literacy students: those who can pay and those who cannot. Those who cannot pay are being educated in community-based programs by teachers who are not licensed. It is argued that these students are being forced to submit to substandard service and back-alley education.

All true literacy teachers are licensed by the state and need to participate in fifty hours of continuing education every year to be relicensed. Licensing was instituted twenty years ago to protect unsuspecting learners from those elementary school teachers with no background in

R. G. Brockett (ed.). *Continuing Education in the Year 2000.*
New Directions for Continuing Education, no. 36. San Francisco: Jossey-Bass, Winter 1987.

continuing education who were operating proprietary adult basic education (ABE) programs. Teachers are certified by the ABE Commission by passing a standardized test for specialty work in math, English, reading, and life-coping skills. Of course, those with subspecialty credentials will be paid more money.

It is now illegal for anyone to take the General Educational Development Test who has not been through continuing education programs. Only the professionals can identify the needs and problems of students. Only continuing education can provide the proper remedy. Only continuing education will know when these people are ready to take the test. Self-instruction will not be tolerated.

Continuing educators would not have to worry about being sued by students who did not pass the test or get a job. These cases are brought before fellow continuing education professionals because only they are competent judges in the arcane and rarefied atmosphere of continuing education. Now that continuing education has finally reached its goal and is recognized as a professional field, a consumer movement has begun to ask the question, does all of this professionalism guarantee that students really learn, or is this simply a charade for continuing educators to increase their occupational status and income?

What Will Be the Future Issues?

If one thinks that this image is unbelievable, one need only remember that a major issue in the Flexner report (1910), which revolutionized medical education in 1910, was whether physicians needed to have a high school diploma. It is unlikely that anyone at the time would have been able to predict the structure of medical education today.

This scenario raises the question of what the field of continuing education should strive to become in the future. This chapter will discuss the most fundamental issues the field will face as it seeks answers to this question. Before going any further, I need to clarify what an issue is and how to identify which will be the most important ones in the year 2000.

What is an issue? First, it may help to define what it is not. There are many problems in continuing education, such as financing. Almost everyone would agree that continuing education needs a better system of financing. With problems there is an agreed-upon end and the discussion focuses on the best means to reach that end. In contrast, an issue is a normative question for which two or more starting points or assumptions exist. Depending on which starting point is used, a different conclusion is reached about the question. Thus, with issues there is conflict about ends as well as means.

Depending on which set of lenses are used to view the field, different types of issues will emerge. In identifying issues that the field will face in the year 2000, it is necessary to circumscribe the context in which these issues will exist. However, the field does not face issues; rather, people who work in the field do. To identify issues, then, I need to describe the types of continuing educators whose future we wish to analyze. In this discussion I will identify issues that will be faced in the year 2000 by people who consider themselves continuing educators.

Continuing educators conceive of themselves as applying a set of skills such as teaching, counseling, program development, or administration within the context of a subfield of practice (Darkenwald and Merriam, 1982). These subfields of practice are defined in terms of either a type of institution such as higher education, business and industry, or libraries, or a programming area such as continuing professional education or adult basic education. The issues that I identify cut across all of these subfields of practice. In fact, this entire discussion presumes there is a field of practice in continuing education that is not tied to an institution or program area. To discuss the issues in this field of practice, we must move one level of abstraction above the subfields. The most fundamental issues at this level of abstraction relate to whether, in people's minds, a field of continuing education actually exists or whether there is a profession of continuing education.

Which issues will be important in the year 2000? Although many issues will be of importance to continuing educators, I have selected two that are being discussed now and that show no signs of being resolved before the year 2000. I consider these issues the most fundamental ones that must be faced. They are, first, whether the field of continuing education should seek to professionalize further and, second, what model of professionalization should be followed? These issues must be discussed and understood because they provide the foundation for all the other issues in the field.

These questions have been intensely discussed by continuing educators for at least the past thirty-five years. In order to fully understand the future of these issues, it is necessary to provide some historical context. In the following sections I present the past and present understandings of these two issues as well as my analysis of the future. Although the two issues are interrelated, I separate them for the analytical part of the chapter and weave them together in my final observations. In the following section, I will consider the first question of whether continuing education should seek to professionalize further.

Should Continuing Education Professionalize?

Before answering this normative question, let us first review the descriptive question of whether continuing education is a profession. The two major approaches used to determine whether an occupation is a profession are represented by Flexner (1915) and Wilensky (1964). Flexner proposes an all-or-nothing approach while Wilensky suggests that occupations exist on a continuum of professionalization. Anyone who has answered this descriptive question has concluded that continuing education is not yet a profession or, in Wilensky's terms, is low on the professionalization continuum.

Royce (1987) has located the first debates on the question in the 1950s. McClusky, as reported in Becker (1956), addressed the question, Is adult education a profession? and answered, "Not yet!" He argued that first, there were not enough clearly defined positions; second, there were not enough standards by which to judge the performance of adult educators; and third, there was not a sufficiently well-defined body of knowledge about adult education. The situation has not changed appreciably twenty-five years later, leading Farmer (1974), Griffith (1980), and Darkenwald and Merriam (1982) to conclude that continuing education has not yet reached professional status but rather is an occupation in the process of becoming professionalized. Darkenwald and Merriam (1982) identified many of the same problems that had been noted by McClusky, such as the limited visibility of the field and lack of career lines, the fact that professional preparation is not usually required for employment as a continuing educator, and a limited knowledge base upon which professional development depends.

There was a debate as early as the 1950s about whether adult education should professionalize further. Liveright indicated that while there is "increasing concern about professionalization of the field . . . the paths toward professionalization are anything but clearly marked . . . [and some] doubt the wisdom of trying to set up adult education as a profession" (1958, p. 67). In speaking for the majority of continuing educators, however, Houle (1956) argued forcefully that the field should seek to professionalize. The majority of continuing educators today concur with Houle that the field should professionalize (Brown, 1984; Cameron, 1981). Darkenwald and Merriam probably capture best the spirit of this viewpoint: "It should no longer be acceptable that anyone at all may lay claim to being an adult educator . . . . Learning by trial and error was a necessary . . . form of professional preparation in the past, but it is not today" (1982, p. 235).

The debate still persists with theorists such as Carlson (1977) and Rothaus (1981) arguing that professionalization is not in the learners' best interests. Darkenwald and Merriam (1982) summarize these arguments by stating that the exclusionary practices and standard setting associated with professionalization are seen as inconsistent with the voluntary and informal nature of continuing education. In the next section I present an analysis for the future discussion of this issue.

An Analysis for the Future: Professionalization, Not Professionalism

Given the variety of definitions of *professionalization*, I must first clarify the one that I am using. However, before proceeding let me offer a note about what I am not talking about. I am not referring to how "professional" an individual is. In common parlance, this term has come to mean a competent, committed worker. Thus, we speak of professional car mechanics, plumbers, and exterminators. If this were the definition, continuing educators would already be as professional as the members of any other occupation.

My unit of analysis must be the occupation rather than the individual because individuals don't professionalize, occupations do. I will use what is considered to be the dominant mode of analysis in the sociological literature to guide the discussion. Larson (1977) says that professionalization is the process by which producers of special services constitute and control the market for their services. For this professional market to exist, a distinctive commodity must be produced. Now, professional work is only a fictitious commodity. Unlike industrial labor, most professions produce intangible goods in that their product is inextricably bound to the person who produces it. It follows, then, that the producers themselves have to be produced if their products are to be given a distinctive form. In other words, professionals must be adequately trained and socialized so as to provide recognizably distinct services for exchange on the professional market.

At this point, it is useful to examine in greater detail the one condition that has been a necessary step in the professionalization of every other occupation. In order to provide a recognizably distinct service, a profession must have a recognizably distinct and standardized knowledge base that is taught to its new members. For most professions the production of knowledge and the production of practitioners are unified into the same structure. That is, the model of research and training institutionalized by the modern university gives to professions the means of controlling their knowledge base as well as to award credentials certifying that the practitioner possesses this recognizably distinct type of knowledge. Therefore, the level of professionalization of an occupation can be assessed by the extent to which its credentials are accepted as necessary to provide a specific type of service.

Using this definition of *professionalization*, we can assess the extent to which various subfields of continuing education have professionalized. Not unexpectedly, the most professionalized subfield is the professoriate. While no data have been systematically collected, a reasonable estimate is that at least 80 percent of the Commission of Professors of Adult Education have earned doctorates in continuing education. Thus, this group has been reasonably successful at constituting and controlling the market for its services. The Commission of Professors is presently discussing a process that can increase its level of professionalization: accreditation standards for graduate programs. This effort to establish a process of accrediting graduate programs in continuing education is simply an attempt to make formal, explicit, and mandatory what has been informal, implicit, and voluntary. It is clear that one goal of these standards is to prohibit anyone without the proper credentials to practice in this subfield of continuing education. If these standards can be successfully implemented, the professoriate will become more highly professionalized.

In examining other subfields, the levels of professionalization drop dramatically. I would argue that a fundamental cause of these low levels is the lack of a recognizably distinct knowledge base. Graduate programs of continuing education universally have problems defending the exclusiveness of their knowledge base. Deans and governing boards have been known to ask what is unique about their graduates and why they cannot obtain a degree in other areas such as instructional technology, educational psychology, administration, or curriculum.

This lack of exclusivity in the knowledge base of continuing education has made it difficult to constitute and control a market for expertise in the specific subfields of practice. For example, 94 percent of the teachers in ABE are certified to teach elementary or secondary education, while only 13 percent of ABE teachers are certified in continuing education (Development Associates, 1980). Sixty-eight percent of deans and directors in continuing higher education have doctorates. Forty-two percent of these doctorates were earned in some field of education other than continuing education, while 33 percent were earned in the liberal arts and sciences (Azzaretto, 1986). The remainder, only 25 percent, are continuing education doctorates. These figures illustrate the first problem in defining and defending a knowledge base in continuing education—that is, differentiating it from other knowledge bases in the field of education. For example, do people trained in continuing education perform any differently in ABE classrooms than certified elementary school teachers? Or, what is the difference between a person trained in continuing education and one trained in higher education? Which one is better qualified to be a dean of continuing education at a university?

The second problem in defending a knowledge base in continuing education is even more fundamental. Do continuing educators have any specialized knowledge that is not possessed by people trained in other disciplines or professional fields? This problem is illustrated by the fact that 33 percent of deans and directors in continuing higher education have their degrees in fields other than education. Continuing professional education (CPE) is another subfield where this problem is particularly evident. Griffith (1985) has estimated that the great majority of continuing professional educators have not been formally trained in education. The dominant view in CPE is that one must be a content expert, such as a physician, lawyer, or minister, in order to direct the continuing education function within that profession.

I expect that a similar situation exists in most, if not all, subfields in continuing education. Except for the professoriate, I would conclude that continuing educators have not managed to constitute and control the market for their services in any subfield of practice.

What about the future? Should continuing education seek to professionalize further? In a recent dissertation, Brown (1984) surveyed a national sample of continuing educators who answered with a resounding yes to this question. Eighty-three percent would like to see the field professionalize further. I see the process of professionalization as very likely to continue. In fact, I truly believe that the normative question about future professionalization of continuing education is hardly worth discussing. Unless all graduate programs in continuing education are dismantled, continuing educators will continue their efforts to constitute and control the market for their services by producing certified continuing educators. The process of professionalization began fifty years ago with the establishment of degree programs in universities. This process is a function of pervasive social, political, and economic forces inherent in Western capitalist societies (Larson, 1977). While we certainly have options as individuals about whether to participate in this process, it is difficult to imagine what other alternatives we have as an occupation. Let us accept our involvement in the process of professionalization and move to the more important issue concerning the options we have in shaping the professionalization of our field. This issue is developed in the following section on models of professionalization.

Models of Professionalization for Continuing Education

As described earlier, there has been a great deal of debate over whether the field of continuing education should seek to professionalize. For those who have argued against accepting the dominant models, an attractive alternative has been to suggest the need to find or create different models of professionalization. Carlson (1977) has stated this most directly: "Are there any viable alternatives to the traditional type of professionalization? . . . a careful search for alternative approaches to professionalization is one of the most important . . . research areas in the field . . . " (pp. 60–61). Hentschel (1981) and Rothaus (1981) suggested that continuing educators seek to develop relationships with learners as equal partners rather than entering into the hierarchical expert-client relationships typical of other professions. Cervero (1985) concluded that, after pointing out the contradictions between the dominant model of professionalization and the "central core of what adult education is all about . . . it is worth working on the task of constructing a 'new vision' of professionalism for our field" (pp. 13, 16). Finally, in her national survey of continuing educators, Brown (1984) concluded that "support for . . . a modified professionalism is viable among adult educators" (p. 150). She went on to say that "the occupation of adult education has an opportunity to develop an alternative model of professionalism" and that the "challenge . . . is to develop an occupational model by sharing power more equally between practitioner and client" (p. 150).

These calls for new models of professionalization must be discussed in the context of similar calls in many other professions. Schon (1983) has argued persuasively for a new kind of professional, one who is a "reflective practitioner." Carroll answered the question posed in his title "The Professional Model of Ministry—Is It Worth Saving?" by saying that it is necessary to "reconceive and reinterpret the professional model to make it more applicable to ordained ministry" (1985, p. 43). Giroux and McLaren (1986) argue for a reconceptualization of the teaching profession to revive the values of democratic citizenship and social justice. Finally, Kissam sees in the decline of law school professionalism the opportunity to "reduce the concepts of legal formalism and legal autonomy to their appropriate, limited places in legal education, and to replace these concepts with a more contextual and more critical study of the legal process" (1986, p. 323). Thus, we see continuing education facing many of the same issues as other, more established professions. With this type of support, it is worth discussing the field's future directions for professionalization.

An Analysis for the Future: Alternate Models of Professionalization

Which models of professionalization are available to continuing educators? I see two very different ways to construct these future models. The first is to professionalize in what many opponents of traditional forms of professionalization consider to be unexamined or unreflective ways. If this type of model were followed, the scenario I described in the opening section of the chapter would be a likely future.

A second option would be to seek alternatives to the model of unreflective professionalization. Before examining these alternate models, let us review what type of support may exist for them. In the previous section, I indicated that a group of continuing educators have urged the field to reject current models of professionalization and to seek alternate ones. Many practitioners seem to support this idea. In Brown's (1984) sample of continuing educators, 56 percent agreed that the field should develop a model of professionalization different from that of medicine.

The major unanswered question, however, has been what alternate professional models might look like. I believe that we have simply not known where to look. Rather than focusing on the process by which continuing educators are certified, we need to focus on how continuing educators use their power and to what ends. While members of a profession may receive a common training, Murphy (1986) has demonstrated that they use this common background for very different personal and social purposes. For example, some clergy see their function only as ensuring the personal salvation of the members of their congregation. In contrast, others, such as those working in the tradition of liberation theology, define their role as improving the material condition of people's lives. Some physicians are refusing to serve the poor and elderly because changes in third-party payment systems have limited the amount that they can be reimbursed under Medicare and Medicaid. On the other hand, some physicians operate free clinics for these groups. Many social workers participate in a process that makes their clients more dependent on the institutions that serve them, while others are involved in political action to change the structural conditions that cause poverty. These examples demonstrate that the ends of professional practice are characterized by diversity and conflict, not consensus. The practice of professionals is a far more diverse phenomenon than the preparation of professionals. The assumption that professions are best understood as communities united by common interests is simply a myth.

We do not need to create alternate models out of thin air. By looking at the practice of continuing education rather than the process of training, we can see many alternate models of professionalization. The field should professionalize in ways that are consistent with central beliefs about what it means to be continuing educators. I would suggest six assumptions that need to be made along the path to professionalization.

First, educators do not seek autonomy in decision making regarding learners' needs or the solutions to those needs. Rather, learners should be involved, both personally and collectively, in determining both needs and solutions.

Second, learning needs should not be treated as deficiencies of the individual that can be treated and remedied. Rather, learning needs should be viewed as adults' right to know. That is, the vision of continuing education should be revised from a medical model to a human rights model.

Third, the larger portion of adults' learning does not require assistance. Continuing educators should not seek to destroy the beauty of friends teaching friends or of self-directed learning. Rather, they must discriminate among situations where assistance would provide more effective learning and where it would not. That is, professional continuing education is not always better than nonprofessional continuing education.

Fourth, continuing educators must recognize that problems that require learning usually do not develop within the individual but rather are a function of the individual within the social-political-economic environment. Thus, individuals and their learning needs cannot be isolated from the circumstances that produced those needs. Continuing educators must help learners solve their problems within a context. Further, they must be careful to discriminate between problems for which education is the appropriate solution and those for which it is not.

Fifth, educators exist in a symbiotic relationship with adult learners. While the learners would probably survive without the educators, the educators could not exist without the learners. Thus, the temptation to create and exploit learning needs to further the interests of continuing education must be avoided.

Sixth, educators are not value-neutral possessors of a technical process. They are political actors within a social structure and their programs always have outcomes that maintain this structure or change it. They must continually review and reassess the ends of their practice, not just the means.

Continuing educators should base their work on these six assumptions. By doing so, they are likely to end up with a professionalized field that is consistent with their fundamental beliefs about continuing education. To the extent that these assumptions do not underlie practice, the field will likely resemble the scenario at the beginning of the chapter.

A Concluding Observation

It is my hope that by the year 2000, continuing education can move beyond the issue of whether it should professionalize. Continuing education has answered this question by engaging in the process of awarding credentials through higher education institutions. Instead, attention should be focused on the issue of which models of professionalization will be followed. My vision is not like the one I sketched for the year 2020. Rather, professionalization should recognize that different, and to some extent competing, purposes, knowledges, and ideologies underlie the work of continuing educators. The very least they can do is to ensure that these differences are represented in the content of graduate training programs and the constituencies of professional associations. They must not trivialize the knowledge and practice of those who work outside the mainstream. They should recognize that the work of peace educators is as valid as that of military educators. They should recognize that the work of educators in community-based literacy programs is as valid as that of publicly funded ABE programs. Finally, they must recognize that continuing educators' work with marginalized members of society, such as the poor and racial minorities, is as valid as that of those who work with dominant groups, such as the professions and businesses. This is the legacy of the beginning of continuing education as a field of practice and it is also the best hope for the future practice of the profession.

References

Azzaretto, J. F. "Survey Results of Continuing Educators for the Professions." Paper presented at the National University Continuing Education Association Conference, Portland, Ore., Apr. 28, 1986.

Becker, H. S. "Some Problems of Professionalization." *Adult Education,* 1956, *6* (2), 101–105.

Brown, C. D. "Ideological Orientation and Attitudes Toward Professionalism Among Adult Educators." Unpublished doctoral dissertation, Northern Illinois University, 1984.

Cameron, C. R. "Certification Should Be Established." In B. W. Kreitlow and Associates (eds.), *Examining Controversies in Adult Education.* San Francisco: Jossey-Bass, 1981.

Carlson, R. A. "Professionalization of Adult Education: An Historical-Philosophical Analysis." *Adult Education,* 1977, *28* (1), 53–63.

Carroll, J. W. "The Professional Model of Ministry—Is It Worth Saving?" *Theological Education,* 1985, *21* (2), 7–48.

Cervero, R. M. "The Predicament of Professionalism for Adult Education." *Adult Literacy and Basic Education,* 1985, *9* (1), 11–17.

Darkenwald, G. G., and Merriam, S. B. *Adult Education: Foundations of Practice.* New York: Harper & Row, 1982.

Development Associates. *An Assessment of the State-Administered Program of the Adult Education Act.* Washington, D.C.: U.S. Department of Education, 1980.

Farmer, J. A., Jr. "Impact of Lifelong Learning on the Professionalization of Adult Education." *Journal of Research and Development in Education,* 1974, *7* (4), 57–67.

Flexner, A. *Medical Education in the United States and Canada.* New York: Carnegie Foundation for the Advancement of Teaching, 1910.

Flexner, A. "Is Social Work a Profession?" *School and Society,* 1915, *1,* 901–911.

Giroux, H. A., and McLaren, P. "Teacher Education and the Politics of Engagement: The Case for Democratic Schooling." *Harvard Educational Review,* 1986, *56* (3), 213–238.

Griffith, W. S. "Personnel Preparation: Is There a Continuing Education Profession?" In H. Alford (ed.), *Power and Conflict in Continuing Education.* Belmont, Calif.: Wadsworth, 1980.

Griffith, W. S. "Persistent Problems and Promising Prospects in Continuing Professional Education." In R. M. Cervero and C. L. Scanlan (eds.), *Problems and Prospects in Continuing Professional Education.* New Directions for Continuing Education, no. 27. San Francisco: Jossey-Bass, 1985.

Hentschel, D. "Growing Up Professional." *Setting the Pace,* 1981, *1* (3), 5–11.

Houle, C. O. "Professional Education for Educators of Adults." *Adult Education,* 1956, *6* (3), 131–141.

Kissam, P. C. "The Decline of Law School Professionalism." *University of Pennsylvania Law Review,* 1986, *134* (2), 251–324.

Larson, M. S. *The Rise of Professionalism.* Berkeley, Calif.: University of California Press, 1977.

Liveright, A. A. "Growing Pains in Adult Education." *Adult Education,* 1958, *8* (2), 67–71.

Murphy, S. "Resistance in the Professions: Adult Education and the New Paradigms of Power." Unpublished doctoral dissertation, Northern Illinois University, 1986.

Rothaus, L. G. "The Conspiracy Against the Laity." *Setting the Pace,* 1981, *1* (3), 16–26.

Royce, S. "Adult Educators and Their Professional Associations: An Analysis of Characteristics, Concerns, and Clientele Needs." Unpublished paper, Teachers College, Columbia University, 1987.

Schon, D. A. *The Reflective Practitioner.* New York: Basic Books, 1983.

Wilensky, H. L. "The Professionalization of Everyone?" *American Journal of Sociology,* 1964, *70* (2), 137–158.

Ronald M. Cervero is associate professor in the Department of
Adult Education at the University of Georgia. His current
research and writing interests are primarily in the area
of continuing professional education. He is a member of the
executive committee of the Commission of Professors of
Adult Education.

*Continuing educators and their constituencies can either be
reactive and learn by shock or be proactive, use techniques
for generating futures perspectives, and influence the
direction of their own future.*

Techniques for Generating Futures Perspectives

David Deshler

There is an increasing recognition on the part of continuing educators
that responding to change, as it rapidly occurs in our society, is not
enough. What is called for is an anticipatory or proactive stance toward
the future, a stance that goes beyond reacting to needs as they occur.
However, this futures orientation toward programming will not be helpful unless it is accompanied by methods and techniques for generating
future perspectives. Continuing educators and their constituencies need
techniques that will provide them with visions of the future that are
more adequate than what can be obtained by looking into a crystal ball.
In jest, we can assert that if we consult crystal balls, we had better get
used to eating crushed glass.

    Some techniques have emerged from research methods to which
the physical, natural, and social sciences have contributed. Others have
come from the world of management in business and industry. Demands
of citizens for technological, environmental, and social risk studies have
required the creation of designs for the assessment of many projects prior
to their being implemented. The use of computers in futures studies has
taught us much about the limitations and possibilities for computer-
generated futures perspectives. A few futurists have contributed approaches that emphasize the importance of intuition, imagination, and
the power of social ideas in shaping the future.

R. G. Brockett (ed.). *Continuing Education in the Year 2000.*
New Directions for Continuing Education, no. 36. San Francisco: Jossey-Bass, Winter 1987.

After reviewing the literature on futures research and action methods, four categories of techniques for generating futures perspectives were identified: anticipatory learning, projection and forecasting, prevention and adaptation, and invention creation. All of these techniques can be used to enhance the capabilities of continuing educators in planning the future of their own educational organizations and programs. In addition, continuing educators can perform a strategic role in promoting the use of these techniques among their learners, their publics, and other organizations in society.

Anticipatory Learning Techniques

The first category includes techniques to increase anticipatory learning. The purpose of these techniques is to overcome resistance to viewing the future; to awaken persons to the necessity of learning to think with a future orientation; to understand the plans, visions, and possibilities that others have created; and to stimulate dialogue concerning decisions about the future. The learning process is aimed at liberating people from socially imposed and unexamined expectations regarding the future, and evaluating ethical and moral decisions that can exert an impact on the future. The major anticipatory learning techniques that have been selected for brief description in this chapter include self-directed learning from futures literature, futures orientation self-assessment, fictional futures discussion and reflection, and the use of futures-oriented games and simulations.

Self-Directed Learning from Futures Literature. Continuing educators can promote anticipatory learning by encouraging self-directed learning from futures literature. Most educators and their publics have already read some popular works and may know about *Futurist* magazine. However, an overview or a guided tour of the literature is essential for the novice. An article by Marien (1983) provides an excellent introduction. After making a distinction between popular fluff versus substantive work, the article describes four recommended literature tours for the novice futures traveler. The first tour recommends several overview books and introductions to the field, including major books on futures research methods. The second tour of futures landscapes focuses on reading one or more works by leading futurists as a way of encountering interesting personalities. Fifty of the most interesting futurist personalities are listed with their literary contributions. The third tour that is recommended is to become familiar with two postindustrial visions of future society: one that emphasizes a service or information society characterized by high technology, material affluence, and leisure, and the other that emphasizes a decentralized, ecologically oriented society characterized by appropriate or intermediate technology. The fourth introductory tour suggests an exploration of special problem areas of future concern. Four or five future-oriented books are listed for each of the following areas: government, cities and housing, transportation, crime and justice, environment and resources, food and agriculture, the economy, work, defense and disarmament, international economics, energy, health, families and children, education, and communications. This article by Marien can provide an introduction for continuing educators and learners as a starting point for their self-directed futures learning projects. However, the *Future Survey*, a monthly abstract of books, articles, and reports concerning forecasts, trends, and ideas about the future, published by the World Future Society (4916 Saint Elmo Avenue, Bethesda, Md. 20814), is probably the best single publication for keeping up with the literature. It is especially helpful in providing abstracts for specific problem areas. All continuing educators should gain access to this publication as the basis for their futures self-directed learning.

Futures-Oriented Self-Assessment. Patton (1986) has designed a self-administered quiz for cooperative extension educators called a Futures Quotient (FQ). This fifteen-item quiz provides specific content for a future-focused role image. Patton summarizes the qualities of an educator who has developed a futurist perspective to include: (1) a balanced perspective—not overly optimistic or overly pessimistic; (2) an empirical perspective—follows statistical trends and qualitative patterns; (3) belief in the possibility of creating the future; (4) innovative—likes to try new things, try on new ideas; (5) intellectually and emotionally stimulated by consideration of futures; (6) a global, universal perspective; (7) comfortable with and challenged by ambiguities, uncertainties, and the unknown; (8) imaginative; (9) modest about, but willing to make, predictions; (10) seeks information from multiple, diverse sources; (11) takes calculated and careful risks; (12) a holistic, big-picture perspective; (13) process-oriented without need for definitive end points and precise answers; (14) creative; and (15) a futurist by self-definition. The use of Patton's FQ or a discussion on the qualities of future-oriented continuing educators could provide a prelude to a strategic planning effort.

Fictional Futures Discussion and Reflection. Another technique for overcoming resistance to viewing the future is to encourage continuing education staff members and their constituencies to engage in reading and discussing fictional futures. This is done not just for entertainment, although it can be that, but for the purpose of viewing our present society through new eyes and for identifying creative ideas for program and curriculum development. Study circles can be organized among people who already read fictional futures literature, thereby adding an educational reflection and discussion dimension to their reading. Parts of continuing education staff meetings could be devoted to reflection and discussion on the implication of future-oriented fiction. Fictional futures also could be used as a prelude to specific planning activities to stretch the imagination of those who are involved in participatory planning.

The fictional futures literature may well be larger than any other type of futures literature. Fortunately there are several reference guides that can be used to make selections and to locate stories that can become the basis for reflection and group discussion for specific situations (for example, Conklin, 1962; Ferman, 1970; Ginsburg, 1970; Asimov, 1971; Calkins and McGhan, 1972; Hollister, 1974; Nicholls, 1979; Barron, 1981).

Games and Simulation Techniques. Although gaming has its origins in military history, gaming for social science or educational purposes emerged during the early 1960s. Games or simulations can be used to build theory, conduct research, or provide learning experiences (McLean, 1978). We are concerned here with games and simulations that can provide anticipatory learning for continuing education personnel and their constituencies.

Examples include Balance, Cope, Dialogues on What Could Be, Ecopolis, Explosion, Futura City, Future Decisions: The I.Q. Game, Futures Planning Maps, Global Futures Game, Ground Zero, Space Future and other cooperative games, Survival, the Game of Future Shock, the Hybrid-Delphi Game, Hopes and Fears Switchboard, the Life-Styles game, the Utopia Game, the World Game, and Utopia. Guides to games and simulations include Horn (1977) and Barney and Wilkins (1986).

Microcomputer software for future-oriented games is increasing. Some of these games help teach a regional, national, and sometimes global perspective on the economy, energy, and the environment. Examples include Market, Monark, Three Mile Island, Energy and Environment, Pollute, International Futures Simulation (IFS), and Simulation: Public Education in Natural Resources Management. Games and simulations also are activities that can bring together youth and adults.

All of the anticipatory learning techniques for generating futures perspectives that have been identified in this section are directed at overcoming resistance to viewing the future. As such, they can assist continuing educators in developing a proactive approach to practice.

Projection and Forecasting Techniques

Another group of techniques for generating perspectives serves projection and forecasting purposes. The usefulness of projection and forecasting is obvious. Obtaining useful projections is more likely if historical precedents exist, regularities of cause and effect are known, quality data are available, and the projected time span is short. The basic assumption underlying forecasting is that each forecaster begins with assumptions about the relationship of the past to the present and then uses records to make projections into the future. Techniques for projection and forecasting that have been selected for brief description in this chapter include Delphi, trend extrapolation, cross-impact analysis, and computer modeling.

Delphi. The word *Delphi* refers to the hallowed site of the most revered oracle in ancient Greece. Legend has it that Apollo was the master of Delphi and was famous throughout Greece for his ability to foresee the future. Those who sought to consult the oracle brought gifts, thereby making Delphi one of the richest and most influential locales in Greece. During the 1950s, the Rand Corporation adopted the name Delphi for an analytic procedure that was developed for assessing expert opinion about the targeting of nuclear weapons. Originally, it was designed to solicit expert opinion on a particular subject through a very structured communication process. Through a series of "rounds," the experts were asked to expound upon a particular matter, respond to other experts' replies, and redefine their own positions anonymously. Today there are a number of different versions to assist both divergent and convergent perspectives on various futures. According to Linstone and Turoff (1975), common procedures or steps include:

1. Form a team to undertake and monitor a Delphi on a given subject.
2. Select one or more panels to participate in the exercise. Customarily, the panelists are experts in the area to be investigated.
3. Develop the first-round Delphi questionnaire.
4. Test the questionnaire for proper wording (for example, ambiguities or vagueness).
5. Transmit the first questionnaires to the panelists.
6. Analyze the first-round responses.
7. Prepare the second-round questionnaires (and possible testing).
8. Transmit the second-round questionnaires to the panelists.
9. Analyze second-round responses (repeat questionnaires and analysis as long as desired or as necessary).
10. Prepare a report by the analysis team to present the conclusions of the exercise.

Whenever the judgments of experts may be helpful, Delphi analysis should be considered to synthesize expert opinion or to generate alternative futures perspectives.

Trend Extrapolation. Trend extrapolation techniques are relatively easy to execute for single indicators when data for several points in time are available (Hill, 1978). Credible projections for events that are subject to regularity can be obtained by using the following steps:

1. Establish the problem of concern and then identify specific indicators that can be indexed numerically.
2. Acquire data on each indicator for several points in time.

3. Plot the data points for each time period on a graph.
4. Analyze the inherent trend by projecting the line on the graph into a future time period, taking into consideration the overall pattern of the line.

Today, statistical packages for microcomputers are making projections more accessible to more groups and organizations.

Cross-Impact Analysis. Cross-impact analysis is a technique used for examining and estimating the interaction among two or more future events (Enzer, 1973; Harrell, 1978; Stover and Gordon, 1978). Cross-impact approaches are used to answer the following basic question: If this event were to occur, what is the probability of other identified events occurring? Responses to this question for each event are recorded on a matrix. The major steps are:

1. Select the events to be included in the analysis.
2. Estimate the initial probability of each event.
3. Estimate the probable influence of each event on other events being considered in a pair.
4. Specify the estimates for each space in the matrix, and then summarize the overall estimates for each event.
5. Interpret the findings.

Posing the relationships among two or more possible events uncovers many other questions and potential relationships for us to consider and to estimate the potential positive, negative, or noneffect on other events.

Promise and Limitations of Computers. It is a common hope that projection and forecasting can be improved with the powerful assistance of computers. Many universities provide access to data bases and computer models for forecasting through their mainframe computers. Often these systems are made available through intra-organization discount telephone lines. Some institutions provide consulting on what is available and how to use it; in urban areas, some libraries offer these services. However, the availability of computer software for forecasting using microcomputers for projection and forecasting has become very attractive to many continuing educators and citizens. Software for agriculture, business, forestry, the environment, population, and many other topics is becoming increasingly available (Barney and Wilkins, 1986).

During the last ten years, advances have been made in the construction of global models using computers to consider the forces that link nations inseparably together—trade, finances, population and migration, climate, rivers, natural resources, pollutant flows, communication, transportation, and treaties. Global modeling scenarios can contribute to our appreciation of what to consider in thinking globally while making decisions locally. The scenarios may focus public opinion on important high-priority issues even if accuracy of forecasting may be limited by unforeseen events that are subject to human error (Meadows, Richardson, and Bruckmann, 1982).

Prevention and Adaptation Techniques

Still other techniques for generating futures perspectives serve prevention and adaptation purposes. The major purpose of these techniques is to prevent potentially undesirable, hazardous, or unintended consequences of past events or present decisions. This assessment activity is especially important when plans to alter the physical or social environment are proposed or specific technologies or policy changes are introduced. The assessment may call for subsequent adaptation, limitation, adjustment, modification, or abandonment of proposals. Techniques for prevention and adaptation that are briefly explained in this chapter include economic, environmental, and social impact assessments, as well as technology and risk assessment.

Economic Impact Assessment. The average citizen is most aware of this type of impact assessment. Newspapers, typically in January, carry economic impact material in categories they think will be of interest. Most major industries conduct these studies for themselves. Often state and federal governments provide reports on the economic impact of specific major economic proposals. Impact assessments are often conducted for employment opportunity, tax and property value changes, tax revenue and local government financial costs, displacement of business, industry and business activity, disruption of community growth, cost of living, standards of living, long-term productivity, energy requirements, and conservation.

Technology Impact Assessment. Today, technology impact assessment goes beyond evaluation of the best design for production to include the identification of present and foreseeable effects and the prevention of negative consequences (Coates, 1978; Boroush, Chen, and Christakis, 1980). Examples of technological categories include military, water supply, disease prevention, food processing, biotechnology, agricultural production, computer and communications, nuclear energy, forest resource, waste treatment, transportation, shoreline and fishing, mining and ocean mineral, and construction and housing.

Environmental Impact Assessment. In the 1960s, environmental risk assessment emerged as a response to technological threats to the environment and was promoted by socially and environmentally concerned groups who were questioning the value of economic gain over environmental preservation. These groups argued that other values were at least equally important as economic growth and these values should be included in policy decisions about economic growth (Manheim, 1984). The environmental movement has shown steady growth in financial contributions to environmental protectionist groups over the last two decades, and the values these groups represent are very strongly held by large sections of the public. Environmental impact assessment has become an integral part of the procedures of all major federal actions significantly affecting the quality of the physical and human environment since the National Environmental Protection Act of 1969, which created the Environmental Protection Agency. More recently, the environmental movement has generated many grass-roots groups that have had positive effects on plans and policies to protect the environment. Most of the federal and state environmental laws enacted in the past few years had no teeth until grass-roots groups went to court to assert the rights of all citizens (Robertson and Lewallen, 1975). The following list contains examples of effect categories that may be required for an environmental risk assessment: air quality, visibility, noise, geography, topography, minerals, soils, water resources, vegetation, wildlife, paleontology, archeological resources, Native American concerns, visual resources, recreation, wilderness, agriculture and forest land use, and transportation.

Social Impact Assessment. During the 1970s, there was widespread recognition that it was not enough to be concerned about the environment while ignoring the social effects of major interventions. Many environmental impact assessments began to include more social impact categories. The National Environmental Protection Act was amended in 1973 to limit harmful effects in many social categories. Effect categories that may be required for social impact assessment include health and safety, variety and diversity of choice, equality of opportunity and benefits, mobility and density of population, displacement of population, human service availability, esthetic value, community cohesion, leisure opportunity, historical continuity, psychological security, neighborhood stability, housing availability and quality, public services, and racial concentrations or diversity. Impact assessments provide:

- An information base for understanding complex effects of proposals such as construction, new products or technologies, new policies and service provisions
- An early warning system to prevent adverse effects
- A tool for citizen groups to use to protect the public's interest and the interests of future generations
- A means of identifying alternative approaches, technologies, and adaptations that are less harmful
- A basis for planning that involves affected constituents.

Value conflicts are inherent in impact assessments. The following trade-offs or decision dilemmas are associated with most impacts: short-term versus long-term costs, tolerable risks and costs versus benefits, decentralized and citizen-controlled technology versus centralized and corporation- or government-controlled technology, benefits to some versus burdens to others, and benefits to present generations versus benefits to future generations. One of the purposes of impact studies is to make these choices manifest. The choices are not all technical, but value-laden and political as well.

Continuing educators can perform several roles in relationship to impact assessments. First, we can become watchdogs to conditions and situations that require impact assessments. Second, we can act as brokers between citizens and organizations that perform impact studies, including colleges and universities, and government agencies. Third, we can disseminate findings from impact assessments to the general public. Fourth, we can facilitate dialogue among interested parties concerning the value bases for decisions.

Invention and Creation Techniques

The fourth category of techniques for generating futures perspectives is invention and creation. The primary focus of these techniques is to challenge existing mental barriers to make use of creative intuition, and to construct visions or plans for a desirable or preferred future. Techniques that serve this purpose assist the users in imagining new possibilities that otherwise would not be considered, due to the human tendency to be bound by what is already known. The major assumption here is that we begin by generating or creating a vision or goal; then we select strategies to fulfill that vision. Techniques selected for this chapter that serve the invention and creation purpose include imaging, scenario creation, futures history writing, and action planning.

Imaging. The purpose of creating images of the future is to enable and motivate persons, families, groups, organizations, and community leaders to invent a future that has not previously existed, to help bring into existence a not-yet-occurred state of affairs, to fashion, create, and design new practices, new institutions, and new ways of being and doing within the context of participants' concerns (Ziegler, 1982). The general procedures summarized from Ziegler (1982, 1985) for imaging include the following steps:

1. Identify the individuals, groups, or organizations who can make a contribution in a process of imaging for the sake of creating a positive future for specific concern.

2. Begin, in a workshop setting, by identifying and focusing on specific concerns each participant has for the future.

3. Clarify participants' concerns through sharing and identifying commonalities so collaboration among those with similar concerns can occur through the rest of the process.

4. Demonstrate that participants can and do image when they remember concrete living images of interesting or important experiences from their own personal past.

5. Generate concrete images of the future in general categories or domains of human experience, such as learning and education, governance, family, religion and spirituality, work, and community. They are not to

interrupt the process by raising practical questions about feasibility, probability, possibility, believability, and politicality at this point in the process.

6. Share images of the future in small groups, giving careful and sensitive listening to others.

7. Initiate the process of focused imaging of the future, identifying and generating clear, concrete, specific images that are anchored with examples of who is doing what, with whom, when, where, how, and why.

8. Receive feedback on focused image descriptions in small groups where listeners receive participants' images and interpret the meaning of what they are hearing. Make analytic, plausibility, and preference judgments.

9. Search the focused images for a central theme or themes that underlie the images; identify those images that are compelling: concrete instances and events of the future that have so captured participants' imagination that they will not be able to dismiss or forget them; and test images.

10. Engage in story-telling time in the large group where participants report their most compelling images on newsprint or flip-chart paper: words, phrases, indicators, songs, dances, diagrams, pictures, and symbols.

11. Form collaboration or imaging teams among those who have discovered central, common, or compatible visions of the future.

Scenario Creation. Scenario creation refers to initially detailed descriptions of the future nature and scope of unfolding potential events, physical objects, and processes. The purpose of a scenario creation is to identify alternative hypothetical series of events or products that could possibly materialize, to test the way the parts fit together, to see insights into events that might otherwise be hidden, to discover interconnections among events and forces, to note the potential effects of macro-events on micro-environments, and to contribute to specific decisions in the present (Wilson, 1978; Ziegler, 1982). The basic steps for the creation of scenarios (Wilkinson, 1983; Ziegler, 1982) are:

1. Set forth a clear, bold, vigorous goal statement for the image or general vision of the future, describing a not-yet-occurred state-of-affairs that the scenario creator proposes to bring about—something that ought to be done or brought into existence.

2. Imagine the indicators that tell the scenario creator or others when the goal will have been achieved.

3. Reflect on and specify the assumptions and rationale that underlie the image, proposed intervention, or plan.

4. Describe and identify those who are affected (benefited, hurt, influenced, changed, left unattended); the implementors (professionals, technicians, financiers, supporters, employees); those who are the policy-makers and decision makers (family members, citizen groups, public offi-

cials, administrators, employers); and, when appropriate, the elements in the physical ecological system.

5. Identify the decisions to be addressed in the planning process.

6. Describe the strategies, means, methods, tools, instruments, or equipment that would be needed to achieve the goal.

7. Select several scenario logics that will give coherence to the scenarios and result in structurally different views of the future, creating alternative scenarios for key decision alternatives that will provide an opportunity to explore the potential consequences of these key decisions.

8. Elaborate a set of scenarios (typically three to five) based on these driving forces and logics. For each scenario, describe how all the relevant macro-environmental forces and decision factors might be affected by the prevailing conditions of that scenario.

9. Identify the decision implications of each scenario, such as the potential opportunities and threats to be weighed in making the decision; the unanticipated consequences, effects, and impact; and the potential scope of them for specific groups.

Scenarios are most helpful in identifying a broad range of forces and potential consequences that should be considered before initiating serious efforts to implement an image or plan.

Futures History Writing. The purpose of futures history writing is to generate conscious awareness of the wide range of events that are likely to link the intended future image or scenario to the present, and to view these in some ordered sequential stages of development. The procedures for Futures History Writing (Ziegler, 1982) are as follows:

1. Through imagination, participants place themselves at a specific point in time in the future, to live a scenario or intended image of the future as a "future present moment." From this stance they are to ask, "How did it happen?"

2. Through the use of their imaginary memory, participants compile a long list of specific concrete instances, events, milestones, stages of development, breakthroughs, changes, and discontinuities in cultural, scientific, political, economic, intellectual, and personal areas.

3. Participants record the items that result from their memory search into a plausible sequence as a historical record, identifying crucial milestones for each of up to seven time periods of four or five years each.

4. Participants review the futures history document for discontinuities and gaps.

5. Participants return to imaging when necessary to create new material for making adjustments and additions.

6. Participants share their futures history documents with others and receive feedback from careful listeners.

7. Participants collaborate in creating futures history documents for scenarios that contain common interests and concerns.

8. Futures history documents are used as springboards for specific action planning. The process can be repeated for alternative scenarios or images of the future to test their desirability, plausibility, and feasibility.

Action Planning. The purpose of action planning is to enable participants in the futures-invention and creation process to begin to take present steps toward their intended futures. The action planning process, according to Ziegler (1982), consists of the following steps:

1. Set short-term, detailed, concrete objectives that will describe movement toward intended futures and are specific to action settings (spaces where something can get done to achieve the objectives).

2. Identify action groups (those who are influenced; those who affect policies, programs, and initiatives; and those who make decisions) necessary to initiate action toward intended futures.

3. Correctly identify and analyze enhancers and inhibitors (forces or factors that affect the entire action process), and select those that can be influenced by participants.

4. Identify resources by naming persons, roles, organizations, institutions, and the actions that each can perform as resources for movement toward intended futures.

5. Design instruments and action by stating clearly who does what, to or for whom, under what conditions or circumstances, with what resources, for what purposes. In addition, to whom, what, and how does accountability occur? What types of evaluation instruments will be used?

The underlying assumption of all the invention and creation techniques for viewing the future is that one begins in the future by envisioning a goal or future state toward which human effort is directed. The present reality is viewed as tethered to the future rather than the reverse. Invention and creation approaches invite us to expand our choices, raise our aspirations, and experience motivation for positive action that imaginative possibilities can bring. Through brainstorming, elimination of obstructive thinking, and reflection on preferences and values, positive goals that attract motivation are created. Invention or creation techniques for viewing the future depend on the capacity to create clear, guiding visions of a preferred, intended future.

Summary

There are few situations where there is immediate clarity regarding which technique to use to generate futures perspectives. Techniques can be adapted, altered, and used in various combinations and sequences. Choice of technique may be related to problem characterization, nature and extent of available information, scope of the situation, urgency of the situation, time frame, and level of participation. Individuals will differ in the importance they place on anticipatory learning, projection and forecasting, prevention and adaptation, and invention and creation. Each cluster of techniques can be viewed as distinct but also as complementary.

In summary, the four alternative methods for generating futures perspectives with their associated techniques may: (1) awaken us to the necessity and benefits of learning to think with a future orientation; (2) challenge us to examine the implications of future trends on our activities and lives; (3) warn us to prevent undesirable, hazardous, or unintended outcomes through appreciating the potential risks and consequences of proposed developments, policies, products, and plans; and (4) help us to invent, create, and focus new visions, possibilities, and goals for a desirable or preferred future that will motivate us, attract resources, and move us to promising action and decision making in the present. These techniques for generating futures perspectives can assist continuing educators in their efforts to clarify their own future mission. Various continuing education publics also can be empowered through being taught how to take proactive stances toward the future.

References

Asimov, I. (ed.). *Where Do We Go From Here?* New York: Doubleday, 1971.

Barney, G. O., and Wilkins, S. *Managing a Nation: The Software Source Book.* Arlington, Va.: Global Studies Center, 1986.

Barron, N. (ed.). *Anatomy of Wonder.* (2nd ed.) New York: Bowker, 1981.

Boroush, M., Chen, K., and Christakis, A. *Technology Assessment: Creative Futures.* New York: Elsevier North-Holland, 1980.

Calkins, E., and McGhan, B. *Teaching Tomorrow: A Handbook of Science Fiction for Teachers.* Dayton, Ohio: Pflaum, 1972.

Coates, J. "Technology Assessment." In J. Fowles (ed.), *Handbook of Futures Research.* Westport, Conn.: Greenwood Press, 1978.

Conklin, G. *Great Science Fiction by Scientists.* New York: Collier, 1962.

Duke, R. D. "Simulation Gaming." In J. Fowles (ed.), *Handbook of Futures Research.* Westport, Conn.: Greenwood Press, 1978.

Educational Film Locator of the Consortium of University Film Centers. (2nd ed.) New York: Bowker, 1980.

Enzer, S. "The Delphi Technique and the Cross-Impact Matrix." In F. Tugwell (ed.), *Search for Alternatives: Public Policy and the Study of the Future.* Cambridge, Mass.: Winthrop, 1973.

Feature Films Directory (8th ed.) New York: Bowker, 1985.

Ferman, E. L. *Twenty Years of the Magazine of Fantasy and Science Fiction.* New York: Putnam, 1970.

Ginsburg, M. *The Ultimate Threshold: A Collection of the Finest Soviet Science Fiction.* New York: Holt, Rinehart & Winston, 1970.

Harrell, A. T. "Cross-Impact Analysis." In A. T. Harrell (ed.), *New Methods in Social Science Research: Policy Sciences and Futures Research.* New York: Praeger, 1978.

Hill, K. "Trend Extrapolation." In J. Fowles (ed.), *Handbook of Futures Research.* Westport, Conn.: Greenwood Press, 1978.

Hollister, B. *Another Tomorrow: A Science Fiction Anthology*. Dayton, Ohio: Pflaum, 1974.

Horn, R. E. (ed.). *The Guide to Simulation Games for Education* (3rd ed.) Cranford, N.J.: Didactic Systems, 1977.

Linstone, H. A., and Turoff, M. (eds.). *The Delphi Method: Techniques and Applications*. Reading, Mass.: Addison-Wesley, 1975.

McLean, J. M. "Simulation Gaming." In J. Fowles (ed.), *Handbook of Futures Research*. Westport, Conn.: Greenwood Press, 1978.

Manheim, P. "The Effect of Social Impact Analysis on Decisions Allocating Investments in Water Resources by U.S. Army Corps of Engineers." Unpublished doctoral dissertation, Cornell University, Ithaca, N.Y., 1984.

Marien, M. "Touring Futures: An Incomplete Guide to the Literature." *The Futurist*, 1983, *17* (2), 12–21.

Meadows, D., Richardson, J., and Bruckmann, G. *Groping in the Dark: The First Decade of Global Modeling*. New York: Wiley, 1982.

Media Collections and Services. New York: Bowker, 1976.

Nicholls, P. *The Science Fiction Encyclopedia*. New York: Doubleday/Dolphin, 1979.

Patton, M. Q. "In Search of Futurists." *Journal of Extension*, 1986, *24*, 24–26.

Robertson, M., and Lewallen, J. (eds.). *The Grass Roots Primer: How to Save Your Piece of the Planet by the People Who Are Already Doing It*. San Francisco: Sierra Club Books, 1975.

Stover, J., and Gordon, T. "Cross-Impact Analysis." In J. Fowles (ed.), *Handbook of Futures Research*. Westport Conn.: Greenwood Press, 1978.

Wilkinson, G. "What We Did and How We Did It." In United Way of America (ed.), *Scenarios: A Tool for Planning in Uncertain Times*. Alexandria, Va.: United Way of America, 1983.

Wilson, I. H. "Scenarios." In J. Fowles (ed.), *Handbook of Futures Research*. Westport, Conn.: Greenwood Press, 1978.

Ziegler, W. A. *Mindbook for the Citizen Leader*. Denver, Colo.: Futures-Invention Associates, 1982.

Ziegler, W. A. *Mindbook for Community Envisioning*. Denver, Colo.: Futures-Invention Associates, 1985.

David Deshler is associate professor of adult and extension education at Cornell University in Ithaca, New York. A more detailed description of techniques in this chapter is found in curriculum materials he and his associates have authored for Working with Our Publics: In-Service Education for Cooperative Extension: Module 8: Techniques for Futures Perspectives *(Washington, D.C.: U.S. Department of Agriculture, Cooperative Extension Service, 1987).*

Several major themes are likely to be predominant as
continuing education nears the year 2000.

Postscript: Toward
the New Century

Ralph G. Brockett

What will the landscape of continuing education look like in the year
2000? The preceding chapters have attempted to provide visions of the
field from several vantage points. As a way of bringing closure to this
sourcebook, several common themes that recur throughout the volume
will be considered. Although the authors approach the future from a variety of perspectives, at least three major themes can be gleaned from the
volume. In addition, three additional considerations for the future that
were implied but not addressed specifically in the previous chapters will
be briefly identified.

A Proactive Approach to Futures Planning

The first theme that is predominant throughout the preceding
chapters centers around the need to take a proactive posture in planning
for the future. From Hiemstra's opening chapter, appropriately entitled
"Creating the Future," through Deshler's discussion of practical techniques for futures planning, each author works from the assumption that
we, as continuing educators, can make choices that will allow us to contribute to a future vision.

Creating the future requires a willingness to plan for the future.

R. G. Brockett (ed.). *Continuing Education in the Year 2000.*
New Directions for Continuing Education, no. 36. San Francisco: Jossey-Bass, Winter 1987.

Ackoff (1974) has distinguished among four attitudes that can be taken toward planning: (1) inactivism, where one assumes a do-nothing posture in the belief that planning will make little difference and may even make things worse; (2) reactivism, where planning is viewed as an exercise in nostalgia in order to recreate the "good old days" of the past; (3) preactivism, where planning involves taking steps to predict and prepare for the future; and (4) interactivism, which is an active effort to direct and shape future directions. While both preactivism and interactivism take an optimistic view of planning for the future, the former position stresses preparation for the future while the latter view emphasizes creation of the future. The authors of this volume have each provided insights that may be useful in the development of an interactive planning philosophy.

Growth of the Continuing Education Field

A second theme found throughout this sourcebook is related to the growth and development of the continuing education field. Hiemstra, for instance, describes the Syracuse Kellogg Project as an effort to link continuing educators through the vast array of resources available within the field. Fay, McCune, and Begin point to a number of societal trends indicative of a clear need for continuing education in the future. Brockett and Darkenwald emphasize the importance of future practice being informed by an expanding research base. And Cervero confronts the issue of professionalization and proposes an alternative vision of the field that will allow for increased strength of continuing education without losing the vitality and freshness that have characterized the field over the past several decades.

Clearly, a major task of continuing educators will be to determine the kind of image the field will project in the year 2000. Most certainly, the field will continue to be characterized by diversity in scope and ideology. Thus, while a single unified vision encompassing all segments of continuing education is probably neither feasible nor desirable, we do need to continue the search for common ground and ways to forge a degree of common identity. If only by virtue of the fact that each of us is concerned with serving the adult learner, some portion of a common vision can help us in drawing from a wider range of resources and perspectives than is possible with a more narrow, highly focused perspective.

Role of Technology

The third theme serving as a common thread throughout the volume is the importance of technology in the future. The development of new forms of media to serve the adult learner is often central to visions of the future. Current developments in such areas as computer technology and home video illustrate how far we have come in just the last several years and provide an indication of the potential pace of future growth. However, as Garrison points out in his chapter, technology is much more than hardware. It is the way in which people use scientific knowledge. For instance, many of the management practices outlined by Smith and planning techniques discussed by Deshler imply the use of technology. Similarly, dissemination of information, as discussed by Hiemstra, and the development of research, as discussed by Brockett and Darkenwald, draw from this broader view of technology. Technology holds the potential of linking continuing education to the larger society through such visions as the "information society" and "high tech/high touch" megatrends discussed by Naisbitt (1982).

Some Further Considerations for the Future

The purpose of this sourcebook has been to address the projected state of continuing education as we enter the new century. The perspectives offered in the previous chapters highlight several of the major areas or issues relevant to the field. In addition, a number of additional themes not specifically discussed can be implied from these chapters. These include preparing future continuing educators, addressing the issue of access, and viewing continuing education in a global context.

Preparing Future Continuing Educators. How will future leaders in continuing education be prepared? Graduate programs in continuing education have grown at a very rapid pace, particularly over the past two decades. However, as Ingham and Hanks (1981) have pointed out, the "inability of the graduate programs in the field to clearly establish the superiority of the university-trained adult educator over the untrained one must be seen as a major failure of our graduate departments" (p. 21). This concern poses a major challenge to those who seek to strengthen graduate preparation in continuing education in the future. Other aspects of preparing continuing educators that may warrant consideration include establishment of undergraduate studies in continuing education, innovation in professional development for continuing educators, and exploration of the roles of professional associations in the field.

Access to Continuing Education Opportunities. Who should continuing education serve? While this question is certainly not a new one, it has particular meaning as we look toward the year 2000. As Fay, McCune, and Begin point out in their chapter, the need and the prospective audience for work-related continuing education will continue to grow. At the same time, we will need to find new and creative ways to break down the barriers to access that have traditionally limited opportunities for those outside of the predominant white, middle-class society.

Continuing education can contribute to either narrowing or widening the educational gaps that exist among sociocultural groups in our society. The choice is ours.

A Global Perspective. A final theme for the future is the need to view continuing education from a global perspective. In a review of adult education literature of the 1970s, Hoare (1982) found that consideration of global issues was limited. Yet, any vision of the future that does not attempt to consider the global context will inevitably be doomed to failure, for it will only be a fragment of a vision. The field of continuing education can ill afford to be concerned only with our own limited domain and still have an impact on the future.

Conclusion

The year 2000 is only a little more than a decade away. Thus, the vast majority of changes that will occur by that time will be the result of efforts made by those practicing in the field today. This is an exciting prospect for it means that practitioners can, and indeed will, have an impact on what the field looks like at the dawn of the new century. By thinking and acting now, steps can be taken to assure that visions become reality.

References

Ackoff, R. L. *Designing the Future.* New York: Wiley, 1974.

Hoare, C. H. "Future Issues in Adult Education: A Review of the Literature of the Seventies." *Adult Education,* 1982, *33* (1), 55–69.

Ingham, R. J., and Hanks, G. "Graduate Degree Programs for Professional Adult Educators." In S. M. Grabowski and Associates (eds.), *Preparing Educators of Adults.* San Francisco: Jossey-Bass, 1981.

Naisbitt, J. *Megatrends.* New York: Warner Books, 1982.

Ralph G. Brockett is assistant professor of adult education at the Center for Adult Learning Research, Montana State University, Bozeman, Montana. He has worked in continuing education for health and human services professionals, served on the executive committee of the Commission of Professors of Adult Education, and is currently book review editor for Adult Education Quarterly.

Index

A

Access: issue of, 95–96; and technology, 42–43
Ackoff, R. L., 94, 96
Action planning, for futures invention, 90
Administration, as managerial function, 59–60
Adult basic education (ABE), and professionalization, 68, 72, 76
Adult Classroom Environment Scale (ACES), 32–33
Adult Educare Bill, 67
Adult learner research: analysis of trends in, 29–40; conclusion on, 37; design of, 36; future, 36–37; history of, 29–30; longitudinal, 36–37; on participation, 33–34; replicating, 37; on self-directed learning, 35–36; on teaching-learning transaction, 30–33
AEDNET, 9–10
Agricultural Extension Service, 5
Apollo, 83
Arnett, J. C., 8, 12
Arthur D. Little Management Education Institute, 23
Asimov, I., 82, 91
Aslanian, C. B., 33, 37
AT&T, and education utility, 20
Austin, N., 60, 64, 66
Azzaretto, J. F., 72, 77

B

Barney, G. O., 82, 84, 91
Barron, N., 82, 91
Becker, H. S., 70, 77
Beder, H. W., 30, 31, 38
Begin, J. P., 1, 15, 27, 94, 95
Bell, C. H., Jr., 24, 25
Bell, D., 3, 12
Bell, W., 4, 12
Bell and Howell, De Vry Institute of Technology of, 23

Bezold, C., 17, 18, 19, 20, 21, 22, 25
Blanchard, K., 64, 66
Boroush, M., 85, 91
Boshier, R. W., 44, 51
Brett, J., 24, 25
Brickell, H. M., 33, 37
Brockett, R. G., 1, 2, 29, 35, 36, 38, 40, 48, 93, 94, 95, 96
Brookfield, S. D., 30, 38
Brown, C. D., 70, 73, 74, 77
Brown, J. S., 46, 53
Bruckmann, G., 84, 92
Brunner, E. de S., 29, 30, 38

C

Calkins, E., 82, 91
Cameron, C. R., 70, 77
Canada, futures activity in, 7
Capital, managing, 57
Carlson, R. A., 70, 73, 77
Carlson, R. J., 17, 18, 19, 20, 21, 22, 25
Carnegie Council on Policy Studies in Higher Education, 16, 25
Carroll, J. W., 74, 77
Carse, J. P., 65, 66
Cassara, B. B., 7, 12
Cervero, R. M., 1, 67, 73–74, 77, 78, 94
Cetron, M. J., 17, 18, 19, 22, 25
Change: and futures planning, 3; and management, 55–56
Chen, K., 85, 91
Cherniss, C., 24, 25
Choate, P., 18, 20, 25
Christakis, A., 85, 91
Clark, R. E., 47, 52
Classroom Environment Scale (CES), 32
Coates, J., 85, 91
Commission of Professors of Adult Education, 7, 71–72
Computer-assisted learning (CAL), and technology, 45–46
Computers, for forecasts, 84
Conklin, G., 82, 91

U.S. POSTAL SERVICE

STATEMENT OF OWNERSHIP, MANAGEMENT AND CIRCULATION
(Required by 39 U.S.C. 3685)

1. TITLE OF PUBLICATION	1A. PUBLICATION NO.	2. DATE OF FILING
New Directions for Continuing Education	4 9 3 - 9 3 0	10/7/87

3. FREQUENCY OF ISSUE	3A. NO. OF ISSUES PUBLISHED ANNUALLY	3B. ANNUAL SUBSCRIPTION PRICE
quarterly	4	$36 indiv/$48 inst

4. COMPLETE MAILING ADDRESS OF KNOWN OFFICE OF PUBLICATION *(Street, City, County, State and ZIP Code) (Not printers)*

433 California St., San Francisco, San Francisco county, CA 94104

5. COMPLETE MAILING ADDRESS OF THE HEADQUARTERS OR GENERAL BUSINESS OFFICES OF THE PUBLISHERS *(Not printers)*

433 California St., San Francisco, San Fran-isco county, CA 94104

6. FULL NAMES AND COMPLETE MAILING ADDRESS OF PUBLISHER, EDITOR, AND MANAGING EDITOR *(This item MUST NOT be blank)*

PUBLISHER *(Name and Complete Mailing Address)*

Jossey-Bass Inc., Publishers, 433 California St., San Francisco CA 94104

EDITOR *(Name and Complete Mailing Address)*

Gordon Darkenwald, Graduate School of Education, Rutgers University, 10 Seminary Pl., New Brunswick NJ 08903

MANAGING EDITOR *(Name and Complete Mailing Address)*

Allen Jossey-Bass, Jossey-Bass Publishers, 433 California St., SF CA 94104

7. OWNER *(If owned by a corporation, its name and address must be stated and also immediately thereunder the names and addresses of stockholders owning or holding 1 percent or more of total amount of stock. If not owned by a corporation, the names and addresses of the individual owners must be given. If owned by a partnership or other unincorporated firm, its name and address, as well as that of each individual must be given. If the publication is published by a nonprofit organization, its name and address must be stated.) (Item must be completed.)*

FULL NAME	COMPLETE MAILING ADDRESS
Jossey-Bass Inc., Publishers	433 California St., SF CA 94104
for names and addresses of stockholders, see attached list	

8. KNOWN BONDHOLDERS, MORTGAGEES, AND OTHER SECURITY HOLDERS OWNING OR HOLDING 1 PERCENT OR MORE OF TOTAL AMOUNT OF BONDS, MORTGAGES OR OTHER SECURITIES *(If there are none, so state)*

FULL NAME	COMPLETE MAILING ADDRESS
same as #7	

9. FOR COMPLETION BY NONPROFIT ORGANIZATIONS AUTHORIZED TO MAIL AT SPECIAL RATES *(Section 411.3, DMM only)*
The purpose, function, and nonprofit status of this organization and the exempt status for Federal income tax purposes *(Check one)*

(1) ☐ HAS NOT CHANGED DURING PRECEDING 12 MONTHS	(2) ☐ HAS CHANGED DURING PRECEDING 12 MONTHS	*(If changed, publisher must submit explanation of change with this statement.)*

10.	EXTENT AND NATURE OF CIRCULATION	AVERAGE NO. COPIES EACH ISSUE DURING PRECEDING 12 MONTHS	ACTUAL NO. COPIES OF SINGLE ISSUE PUBLISHED NEAREST TO FILING DATE
A.	TOTAL NO. COPIES *(Net Press Run)*	1300	1398
B.	PAID CIRCULATION		
1.	SALES THROUGH DEALERS AND CARRIERS, STREET VENDORS AND COUNTER SALES	273	181
2.	MAIL SUBSCRIPTION	607	641
C.	TOTAL PAID CIRCULATION *(Sum of 10B1 and 10B2)*	880	822
D.	FREE DISTRIBUTION BY MAIL, CARRIER OR OTHER MEANS SAMPLES, COMPLEMENTARY, AND OTHER FREE COPIES	98	208
E.	TOTAL DISTRIBUTION *(Sum of C and D)*	978	1030
F.	COPIES NOT DISTRIBUTED		
1.	OFFICE USE, LEFT OVER, UNACCOUNTED, SPOILED AFTER PRINTING	322	368
2.	RETURN FROM NEWS AGENTS		
G.	TOTAL *(Sum of E, F1 and 2 - should equal net press run shown in A)*	1300	1398

11. I certify that the statements made by me above are correct and complete	SIGNATURE AND TITLE OF EDITOR, PUBLISHER, BUSINESS MANAGER, OR OWNER *(signature)* Vice-President

PS Form 3526, July 1984   *(See instruction on reverse)*   *(Page 1)*